WILLIAM FAULKNER AND THE TANGIBLE PAST

William Faulkner

and the

Tangible Past

THE ARCHITECTURE OF YOKNAPATAWPHA

Thomas S. Hines

University of California Press   *Berkeley*   *Los Angeles*   *London*

The publisher gratefully acknowledges the contribution provided by the Art Book Endowment

Fund of the Associates of the University of California Press, which is supported by a major gift

from the Ahmanson Foundation.

University of California Press
Berkeley and Los Angeles, California

University of California Press, Ltd.
London, England

© 1996 by
The Regents of the University of California

Library of Congress Cataloging-in-Publication Data

Hines, Thomas S.
   William Faulkner and the tangible past : the architecture of Yoknapatawpha / Thomas S. Hines.
     p. cm.
   Includes bibliographical references and index.
   ISBN 0-520-20293-7 (alk. paper)
    1. Faulkner, William, 1897–1962—Knowledge—Architecture.
  2. Art and literature—Mississippi—History—20th century.
  3. Faulkner, William, 1897–1962—Knowledge—History.
  4. Yoknapatawpha County (Imaginary place). 5. Architecture,
American—Mississippi. 6. Architecture in literature.
  7. Mississippi—In literature. I. Title. II. Series.
PS3511.A86Z7876 1996
   813'.52—dc20   95-52565
                                CIP

Printed in the United States of America
9 8 7 6 5 4 3 2

FRONTISPIECE
William Faulkner, photograph by J. R. Cofield (1931).

This book is dedicated to my sunny California

children, Taylor and Tracy, in the hope it will

remind them that they are also children of

Yoknapatawpha.

CONTENTS

ILLUSTRATIONS

A C K N O W L E D G M E N T S

Those to whom I am most indebted for inspiring this book are named in the Preface and Appendix A. Those who read the manuscript and offered advice and encouragement include Ann Abadie, Nicholas Adams, Joseph Blotner, Margaret Love Denman, Ronald Filson, Harriett Gold, William Hamer, Kathleen Komar, Karl Morrison, Hubert McAlexander, Marjorie Perloff, John Pilkington, Eric Sundquist, Joel Williamson, and Patricia Brown Young. I am also grateful to the anonymous scholars who read the manuscript for the University of California Press and recommended its publication.

Others furnished different kinds of help and encouragement: B. B. Bradley, Hines Bostwick, Robert Canizaro, Tommy Covington, Howard Duvall, Regina Fadiman, Dorothy Hines, Sally Hines, Robert Ivy, Patty Lewis, William Lewis, Donlyn Lyndon, Mattie Spight McDowell, Henry Mitchell, Rebecca O'Hara, Alan Onoye, Taylor Pointer, Tom Rankin, Andrew Smith, Dorothy Lee Tatum, Richard Weinstein, Meta Carpenter Wilde, Mary Rose Wilds, Jack Case Wilson, Peter Wrobel, and my students and colleagues at UCLA.

I am particularly indebted to Random House and to the American Play Company, representing Jill Faulkner Summers, for permission to quote and reproduce Faulkner's work, and to the editors, designers, and other staff of the University of California Press who patiently helped turn my efforts into a beautiful book.

T.S.H.

Los Angeles

1995

As with most books, the genesis of this one is a complex mixture of lifelong interests, connections, and contingencies. But this book is more personal than most. I was born and spent a significant part of my youth in Oxford, Mississippi, where I had the pleasure of occasional encounters with William Faulkner, a distant relative on my father's side. Both families had come originally from Ripley, Mississippi, some fifty miles to the northeast in the neighboring county of Tippah. I include as an appendix a recent letter to my son, in which I recall my acquaintanceship with Faulkner and the long connections of our family with his. Some readers may prefer to read this letter first.

From my father and his family, I imbibed a passion for history, particularly of the South and of what Faulkner called our *own little postage stamp of native soil* in north Mississippi. As an undergraduate history major at the University of Mississippi, this interest was confirmed to the point that I decided that I wanted to read, write, and teach history as my life's work and to pursue a Ph.D. at the University of Wisconsin, Madison. There, while majoring in American social, cultural, and intellectual history, I minored in art history, specializing in the history of architecture. The latter pursuit helped confirm another childhood passion, largely engendered by my mother, for the built environment and what would come to be called "material culture."

Though she gained local renown as a first-grade schoolteacher, my mother was secretly an architect manqué, gently trespassing, with me in tow, building sites throughout our region whenever they came to her attention. I remember still her thoughtful critiques of the works in progress. For her time and place, she had a sophisticated sense of space and design, which she enthusiastically communicated to me. She was also a knowledgeable collector and arranger of furniture and objects, and I recall the frequent screeching of automobile tires as we would stop suddenly to cruise antique and thrift shops. I was cautioned not to touch, but of course I always did. Stimulated by my penchant for architecture and its accoutrements, I also developed an early interest in photography and began, as a teenager, what would become a lifelong pursuit of documenting the built environment, particularly that of north Mississippi. Over three-fourths of the photographs in this book are mine.

At Wisconsin and later at UCLA, where I began teaching in 1968, my early devotion to southern history and literature waned in deference to my growing commitment to the social and cultural history of architecture. My first book, *Burnham of Chicago: Architect and Planner* (1974), focused on late nineteenth- and early twentieth-century issues involving the rise of the skyscraper and the birth of modern American city planning. In *Richard Neutra and the Search for Modern Architecture* (1982), I analyzed the development of early and middle twentieth-century modernism in Europe and America. Its publication coincided with a Neutra exhibition I cocurated with Arthur Drexler at New York's Museum of Modern Art, a show that traveled for two years to venues on both sides of the Atlantic.

Then, in the mid-1980s, as a respite from these endeavors, I decided to take what I thought would be a break from architecture, to clear my head by immersing myself in something different. For that "something," I chose a serious but relaxed reexamination of Faulkner, rereading in ripe middle age the novels and stories I had devoured in my twenties, though certainly then with less than total comprehension. Now, with an additional quarter century of reading, writing, and living behind me, I began, without other conscious agenda, to reexperience the achievement of America's greatest writer. But, as a good Calvinist boy, as a diligent son of the Protestant work ethic, I soon realized that I could never take on so vast a project just for fun, and to assuage my guilt for such happy self-indulgence I began—furtively at first, then more consciously and aggressively—to underline the architectural passages and references.

Then my compulsive academic superego took over and reminded me of the possibility—indeed the imperative—of doing a "nice little article" on Faulkner's architecture. This momentum was adventitiously encouraged by an invitation from the University of Mississippi Center for the Study of Southern Culture to attend the annual August "Faulkner and Yoknapatawpha" conference and to lead an architecture tour of the town and the county. I was also asked to give a short talk on the subject, which led in 1988 to an article in *PLACES: A Quarterly Journal of Environmental Design*. That, I assumed, was the end of an enriching diversion, and I returned to an earlier commitment to write a series of essays, and ultimately a book, on modernist architectural culture in Southern California. Yet again, my trajectory was happily interrupted by another invitation from the Center for the Study of Southern Culture, this time to develop a larger paper on the architecture of Yoknapatawpha for the 1993 conference on "Faulkner and the Artist." This inspired another round of rereading and rethinking, with encouragement from various fronts—including, most importantly, the University of California Press—to expand my paper into a book.

In all successive versions of this project, from the beginning paper to its present incarnation, I have taken as a model the approach of the critic Malcolm Cowley in his epochal anthology *The Portable Faulkner,* first published by Viking in 1946, when most of the author's work was no longer in print. What Cowley did, with Faulkner's consent, was to take apart the oeuvre and put selected pieces of it together again in the form of a compressed, though still sprawling, *chronological* saga. That is, of course, a method and an attitude that is logical and congenial to me and most historians. Like Cowley, I have disassembled and reassembled Faulkner's work in a roughly chronological way, though here with an emphasis on architecture and the built environment. Though I illustrate my ideas with specific examples, this essay does *not* purport to be an encyclopedic history of north Mississippi architecture. Neither does it attempt to cover every reference to architecture in Faulkner's novels and stories or to evaluate the role of architecture in each particular work. To avoid redundancy in this short book, many vivid images were reluctantly passed over. This is a study of how the built environment served Faulkner as background and foreground, as symbol and subject, in the long, grand, diachronic sweep of the Yoknapatawpha narrative. In this pursuit, I have quarried not only major works, such as *Absalom, Absalom!*, but such lesser achievements as *Mosquitoes* and *Knight's Gambit*, to document the pervasiveness of architecture in Faulkner's thinking as a whole. This book explores Faulkner's use of architecture and its accoutrements, not only as another way of understanding Faulkner's work, but as a way of appreciating the power of architecture to shape and reflect what Faulkner, himself, called *the comedy and tragedy of being alive.*[1]

PLATE I

John McCready, "Oxford on the Hill" (1939). City Hall,
Oxford, Mississippi.

PLATE 2
Dogtrot House, Lafayette County, Mississippi (late nineteenth
century, demolished).

PLATE 3

Dogtrot House, Lafayette County, Mississippi (late nineteenth century, demolished).

PLATE 4

Above: Jones House, Lafayette County, Mississippi (mid-1850s, demolished).

PLATE 5

Opposite: Shipp House, Lafayette County, Mississippi (ca. 1857, demolished).

PLATE 6

Above: Neilson-Culley House, Oxford, Mississippi, attributed to William Turner, architect (1859).

PLATE 7

Opposite: St. Peter's Episcopal Church, Oxford, Mississippi, attributed to Richard Upjohn, architect (1859).

PLATE 8
Airliewood, Holly Springs, Mississippi (ca. 1858).

PLATE 9

Pegues House, Oxford, Mississippi, Calvert Vaux, architect
(1859).

Old Federal Building (1885) and double-porched structures leading to Courthouse Square, Oxford, Mississippi.

Introduction

"TIME AND ITS FURNITURE"

In Faulkner's second novel, *Mosquitoes*, a character *leaned nearer to see the paper. It was a single sheet of a Sunday magazine section: a depressing looking article in small print about Romanesque architecture. . . . "Are you interested in architecture?" she asked intensely. . . . "So many people waste their time over things like architecture and such. It's much better to be a part of life, don't you think . . . than to make your life barren through dedicating it to an improbable and ungrateful posterity. Don't you think so?" "I hadn't thought about it." Pete said cautiously.* [1]

Yet Faulkner clearly *had* thought about it. He believed that the art of architecture—like the art of literature—was indeed a "part of life" and did contribute to the culture and civilization of a not "ungrateful posterity." Architecture was important to Faulkner personally. He had an eye and a feeling for the form, function, and meaning of buildings in his actual surroundings, and he used those elements of his Mississippi environment as the models for the architecture of his invented world: the town of "Jefferson" and the county of "Yoknapatawpha." He gave five of his novels titles with architectural implications: *Sanctuary, Pylon, The Hamlet, The Mansion,* and *The Town.* The original, discarded title of both *Light in August* and *Absalom, Absalom!* was *Dark House.* Many of his stories have architecturally suggestive titles and themes, and architects appear as characters and symbols throughout the work.

Faulkner's fellow Mississippian Eudora Welty once insisted that "place has a more lasting identity than we have . . . fiction depends for its life on place. Location is the cross-roads of circumstance." And of all the masters in the history of literature, Faulkner was one of the greatest in his ability to see, to evoke, to explicate, to use the details and the essences of the physical environment. In his sense of place, of genius loci, he was equalled, in the English-speaking world, only by Thomas Hardy, James Joyce, and Henry James. "It sometimes seems to me," observed Malcolm Cowley of Yoknapatawpha in *The Portable Faulkner,* "that every house or hovel has been described in one of Faulkner's novels."[2]

Much has been said and written on the ubiquity of nature in Faulkner's work—the woods, the bear, the natural landscape—but relatively little has been done on Faulkner's equally great interest in the *built* environment, the opposite of nature, as symbol and metaphor of larger issues, attitudes, and moods. There is, in fact, throughout Faulkner criticism a puzzling imbalance between the attention given to nature and that given to architecture. This is unfortunate, since "novelistic architecture," according to critic William Ruzicka, "has much to say about the way that characters view the world they inhabit, the effect of the fictive environment upon those who live within it, the image and significance of a fictive place, and the meaning of dwelling there."[3]

Historian Joel Williamson recognized that "Faulkner early evolved a symbology in which buildings stood for artificial, man-made institutions and the 'outdoors' stood for the natural order. In his stories, doors and door frames, windows and window frames became especially important. His characters were forever looking in or looking out, crawling in or crawling out of windows. They passed in and out of doors, faced closed doors and locked doors, and plunged through, paused, rested, or sat in doorways. Very often to go into a house or building was to attempt to enter the modern world and deal with it on its own terms, to go out was to abandon that effort and seek salvation in nature. Stairs, porches, chimneys, and attics also had easily understood meanings."[4] Yet it could also be argued that nature in Faulkner often represents not order but rather its opposite, and that to escape nature's wild and scary chaos, one could sometimes find shelter and comfort only in architecture and the built environment, which in fact seem to stand for order, sanity, and serenity. On another level, instead of representing the "modern world," architecture, particularly older buildings, could seem in Faulkner's cosmos to be a protective retreat from the stressful demands of modern life.

While cultural and architectural historians have done reasonable justice to the certified monuments and the great urban centers, they have had more trouble getting at the essence of the small, rural, parochial places. Perhaps Faulkner and other writers of what is called "fiction" can, through their particular kind of imaginative probing, help to locate and explicate the sense and meaning, the smell and ambience of the more elusive, more anonymous architectures of the "Jeffersons" of the world.

The historian Hayden White has made useful observations on the problems of literary classification and overclassification. Historians, he acknowledges, are concerned primarily with events that were at some point observable or perceivable and which can be assigned to a specific time and place, whereas "imaginative" writers—poets, playwrights, and especially novelists—are concerned with those kinds of events as well as imagined or invented ones. White insists that "viewed simply as verbal artifacts, histories and novels are indistinguishable from one another . . . unless we approach them with specific preconceptions about the kinds of truths that each is supposed to deal in. But the aim of the writer of a novel must be the same as that of the writer of a history. Both wish to provide a verbal image of 'reality.' The novelist may present his notion of this reality indirectly, that is to say, by figurative techniques, rather than directly, which is to say, by registering a series of propositions which are supposed to correspond point by point to some extratextual domain of occurrence or happening, as the historian claims to do. But the image of reality which the novelist thus constructs is meant to correspond in its general outline to some domain of human experience which is no less 'real' than that referred to by the historian. It is not then a matter of conflict between two kinds of truth," White concludes, between the historian's truth of correspondence and the novelist's truth of coherence. "Every history must meet standards of coherence no less than those of correspondence if it is to pass as a plausible account of 'the way things *really* were.'" A similar duality is suggested in the title, and the text, of an article by the psychoanalyst and historian Erik Erikson: "Psychological Reality and Historical Actuality." [5]

Still, Faulkner's Chick Mallison, in *Knight's Gambit,* may have been speaking for the author himself in his obvious partiality to the truth-telling prerogatives of fiction. It was, he asserted, *only in literature that the paradoxical . . . anecdotes in the history of a human heart can be juxtaposed and annealed by art into verisimilitude and credibility.* Speaking in the voice of another alter ego, Faulkner confirmed this sentiment by insisting that *poets are almost always wrong about facts. That's because they are not really interested in facts: only in truth: which is why the truth they speak is so true that even those who hate poets by simple natural instinct are exalted and terrified by it.* [6]

Whatever the relative significance of nature and architecture in Faulkner's world, the element that most pervaded his cosmos and his consciousness, that both linked and differentiated nature and architecture, was the crucial element of time, or of what physicist Albert Einstein in his theory of relativity called "the fourth dimension." Faulkner's obsession with time was in fact the quality that most linked him with history and which, in turn, has most attracted historians to his work. While history has been called the most eclectic of disciplines, substantively and methodologically exploiting whatever seems to provide that necessary quotient of coherence and correspondence, the medium, the essence, the sine qua non of historical enquiry, the element that distinguishes it from all other disciplines, is its commitment to the primacy of time and its attributes: sequence, precedence, and consequence.

Critic Elizabeth Kerr has observed that philosopher Henri Bergson's concept of time, which Faulkner acknowledged as applicable to his own, underlay the novelist's fusion of past and present and "prevented him from conceiving of different periods as discrete units. The tendency of the South to live in the past and to be preoccupied with family and tradition may have predisposed Faulkner to feel that *no man is himself, he is the sum of his past. There is no such thing really as was because the past is.*"[7]

As compared, moreover, with the Bergsonian insistence on the undifferentiated flux of time, the philosopher Gaston Bachelard in *The Poetics of Space* linked time *with* space in a manner with which Faulkner should have felt an even greater affinity. As an auxiliary branch of psychoanalysis Bachelard coined and defined the term "topoanalysis" as "the systematic psychological study of the sites of our intimate lives. In the theater of the past that is constituted by memory, the stage setting maintains the characters in their dominant roles. At times we think we know ourselves in time, when all we know is a sequence of fixations in the spaces of the being's stability—a being who does not want to melt away and who, even in the past, when he sets out in search of things past, wants time to 'suspend' its flight. In its countless alveoli, space contains compressed time. That is what space is for." And in a related sentiment from *Sartoris,* Faulkner had Narcissa Benbow muse upon the prematurely shortened life of young John Sartoris, killed in a plane crash. He had, she thought, *not waited for Time and its furniture to teach him that the end of wisdom is to dream high enough not to lose the dream in the seeking of it.* As one of Faulkner's more pregnant phrases, *time and its furniture* held prescient implications for the relationship in his world of time *and* architecture.[8]

Furniture itself also intrigued Faulkner as a poignant reminder of complex historical currents. Patricia Brown Young, for example, the daughter of his close Oxford friends Ross and Maggie Brown, still slept in the four-poster bed in which her great-great-grandmother, Minerva Hynes Cook, had died from the gunshot wound inflicted by a Union soldier, who had invaded her home near Vicksburg on April 3, 1865. A large bullet hole in the bed's headboard silently testified to the violent event. In 1954, Faulkner made a point of taking a visiting northern friend out in the country to the Youngs' house to show him the bed. Pointing to the bullet hole, he remarked to the visitor: *This is why the war will never be over. This happened to this girl's family.*[9]

As opposed to the relative atemporality of nature, architecture and its accoutrements possessed for Faulkner the qualities of both temporality *and* timelessness. On the one hand, architecture was drenched with time; on the other, it transcended time. Indeed, for a writer as obsessed with time as Faulkner—the passage of time, the loss of time, the crisscross of time, the presence of the past in the present—architecture offered (if not a stopping of time or prolongation of time) at least a way of carrying through time, of projecting over time, a very tangible part of the past. As with other symbols that critics have found in his work, Faulkner's use of architectural symbols was partly conscious and partly an indirect by-product of other intentions as he told his story and said what he had to say.

Faulkner, of course, was an architect of books, not of buildings, and he appreciated the fact that literature and architecture were different art forms in their tangible relationship both to "psychological reality" and to "historical actuality." Nevertheless, he saw and used architecture *as* the tangible past, the visible past, the tangible document of time suspended and continued. Buildings, he knew, were designed, constructed, observed, and used by particular people in particular times and places, but he also knew that, if preserved and cared for, they could outlast the generations that brought them into being, the generations for whom they stood as monuments and markers of identity.

One

"THE PURLIEUS OF ELEGANCE"

The Development of Faulkner's Architectural Consciousness

He was born William Cuthbert Falkner on September 25, 1897, in New Albany, Mississippi, east of Oxford, where his father was working for the family-owned railroad, founded by his great-grandfather, William Clark Falkner, for whom he was named. In the 1920s, for reasons that have never become entirely clear, the second William added a "u" to the family surname. Soon after his birth, the family moved back to Ripley, the ancestral home, northeast of Oxford, where they lived for four years, and then in 1902, when William was five, they moved permanently to Oxford (Fig. 1). After moving through Oxford's public schools, he briefly attended the University of Mississippi and there, to his friend and classmate Ben Wasson, he indicated his already well-formed interest in the observation and criticism of architecture. "More than once," Wasson recalled, "Faulkner pointed out to me the 'bastard qualities' of the [Ole Miss] buildings and said that the Lyceum Building was the best on the campus" (Fig. 2). With *its good overall Greek quality,* Faulkner declared, it possessed *purity and serenity.* In this vein, Faulkner must also have admired the Palladian elegance of the nearby Barnard Observatory (1859; Fig. 3).[1]

Faulkner then left Oxford and ventured out, first to Canada during World War I, then briefly to New Orleans in the early 1920s, and then in 1925 to Europe, where he had a traditional *Wanderjahr* with his friend, the architect William Spratling. Spratling had been commissioned to do sketches of various European buildings for publication in *Architectural Forum,* and Faulkner was with him on many of those expeditions, ob-

FIGURE I

Trigg-Doyle-Falkner House, Fa[u]lkner's childhood home, Oxford, Mississippi (ca. 1855; photograph ca. 1904). WF on pony;
seated l. to r.: his cousin Sally Murry Wilkins and his brothers
John and Murry.

WILLIAM FAULKNER AND THE TANGIBLE PAST

serving the buildings and the drawings in progress. The trip abroad affected him greatly and would show up in his work the rest of his life.[2]

From Milan, for example, he sent his mother a postcard describing the Piazza del Duomo in words that he would later use, almost verbatim, in the long story "Elmer" (Fig. 4). It was an early example of Faulkner's talent for interpreting architectural mood and detail: They *sat drinking beer within the shadow of the cathedral, gazing upward among its mute and musical flanks from which long-bodied, doglike gargoyles strained yapping in a soundless, gleeful derision, where niched were mitred cardinals like Assyrian kings and lean martyrs pierced dying in eternal ecstasy and young unhelmeted knights staring into space.*[3]

Faulkner's memories of Paris would also find their way into several stories and especially into the poignant last pages of *Sanctuary,* where he demonstrated his consciousness of the city's physical and cultural landscape, as his doomed heroine, Temple Drake, sat pondering her stained Mississippi past: *It had been a gray day, a gray summer, a gray year. On the street old men wore overcoats, and in the Luxembourg Gardens . . . the women sat knitting in shawls and even the men playing croquet played in coats and capes, and in the sad gloom of the chestnut trees the dry click of balls, the random shouts of children, had that quality of autumn, gallant and evanescent and forlorn. From beyond the circle with its spurious Greek balustrade, clotted with movement filled with a gray light of the same color and texture as the water which the fountain played into the pool, came a steady crash of music.*[4]

Upon returning to America, Faulkner lived a while longer in New Orleans, where he was especially influenced by the older writer Sherwood Anderson, then living in the French Quarter. In his second novel, *Mosquitoes,* a satire on the habitués of his and Anderson's circle, the young writer composed occasionally resonant sentences that predicted the Faulkner to come, especially in his keen attention to architecture: *Outside the window, New Orleans, the vieux carré, brooded in a faintly tarnished languor, like an aging*

FIGURE 2

Opposite, top: Lyceum Building, University of Mississippi, Oxford, Mississippi, William Nichols, architect (1848).

FIGURE 3

Opposite, bottom: Barnard Observatory, University of Mississippi, Oxford, Mississippi, F. A. P. Barnard, designer (1859).

yet still beautiful courtesan in a smokefilled room, avid yet weary too of ardent ways (Fig. 5). In a related passage, a character peered across Jackson Square, *across stenciled palms and Andrew Jackson in childish effigy bestriding the terrific, arrested plunge of his curly, balanced horse, toward the long . . . Pontalba building and three spires of the cathedral graduated by perspective, pure and slumberous beneath the decadent languor of August and evening* (Fig. 6).[5]

Much later in his career, though earlier in Yoknapatawpha's history, Faulkner trenchantly contrasted the mid-nineteenth-century sophistication of urbane New Orleans with that of neighboring backwoods Mississippi, when in *Absalom, Absalom!* young Henry Sutpen visits the city with his University of Mississippi classmate, Charles Bon, his soul mate, half-brother, and probable lover. In densely erotic and seductive prose, which confirmed a decade's progression in his art, Faulkner evoked the way that the exotic Charles took *the innocent and negative plate of Henry's provincial soul and intellect and exposed it by slow degrees to this esoteric milieu, building gradually toward the picture which he desired it to retain, accept. I can see him corrupting Henry gradually into the purlieus of elegance, with no foreword, no warning, the postulation to come after the fact, exposing Henry slowly to the surface aspect—the architecture a little curious, a little femininely flamboyant and therefore to Henry opulent, sensuous, sinful; the inference of great and easy wealth measured by steamboat loads in place of a tedious inching of sweating human figures across cotton fields; the flash and glitter of myriad carriage wheels, in which women, enthroned and immobile and passing rapidly across the vision, appeared like painted portraits beside men in linen a little finer and diamonds a little brighter and in broadcloth a little trimmer and with hats raked a little more above faces a little more darkly swaggering than any Henry had ever seen before. . . .*[6]

Anderson recognized Faulkner's talent, but he doubted that the city was his metier. "You're a country boy," he told him, and "all you know is that little patch up there in Mississippi where you started from" (Plate 1, Fig. 7). And long after that, Faulkner indeed realized that *my own little postage stamp of native soil was worth writing about and that I would never live long enough to exhaust it, and by sublimating the actual into apocryphal, I would have complete liberty to use whatever talent I might have to its absolute top* (Fig. 8).[7]

FIGURE 5

Above: French Quarter, New Orleans, Louisiana (late eighteenth, early nineteenth centuries).

WILLIAM FAULKNER AND THE TANGIBLE PAST

FIGURE 6

Opposite, bottom: St. Louis Cathedral, Jackson Square, New Orleans, Louisiana (late eighteenth, early nineteenth centuries).

FIGURE 7

Above: Oxford, Mississippi, aerial view, Phil Mullen, photographer (1946).

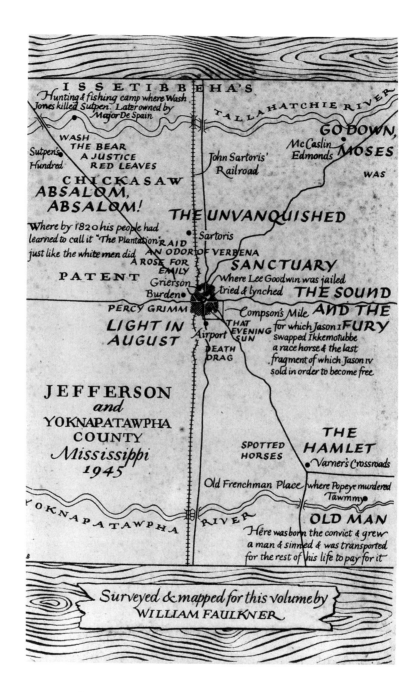

William Faulkner, Map of Jefferson and Yoknapatawpha County, Mississippi (from the *Viking Portable Faulkner,* 1946).

With his third novel, *Sartoris,* Faulkner half-consciously began his Yoknapatawpha chronicle. One of the most vivid areas in which he sublimated *the actual into apocryphal* in that novel and throughout the saga was in the realm of architecture, landscape, and material culture. Indeed, in his long oeuvre, his treatment of architecture encompassed six large categories: folk vernacular, neoclassical, neo-Gothic, High Victorian, and modernist, as well as the related art of public sculpture. In those categories, Faulkner used architecture to help him center and focus his narrative, to evoke mood and ambience, to demarcate caste and class, and to delineate character.

Two

"A JUST AND HOLY CAUSE"

The Public Sculpture of Yoknapatawpha

Though not "architectural" in the sense of providing shelter and functional accommodations, public sculpture was a crucial genre of the Yoknapatawpha landscape. The Confederate Monument, on the Oxford and Jefferson squares, dedicated in the early twentieth century to "those who died in a just and holy cause" faced south from the courthouse and became for Faulkner a crucial symbol in work after work, as in *Sartoris,* where *the Confederate soldier stood, his musket at order arms, shading his carven eyes with his stone hand* (Fig. 9).[1] There is here a curious relationship between the actual and the apocryphal, since Faulkner's words do not literally describe the statue that is on the Oxford Square, but do describe the one that is on the Ole Miss campus a mile away (Fig. 10). This monument, which Faulkner knew as well as he knew the one in town, contained an inscription from Herodotus, in Greek, which he never used but should have liked: "Go, stranger, and to Sparta tell, that here, obeying her commands, we fell."

Oxford is, in fact, one of the few small Southern towns with two Confederate monuments, a result of a compromise between two warring factions of the United Daughters of the Confederacy, one group wanting the statue placed on the square, the other arguing that it should be on the campus. One of the UDC members who took part in the battle was Faulkner's own grandmother, the wife of J. W. T. Falkner. The grandson evoked one aspect of the conflict in *Requiem for a Nun,* where the monument was seen both to shape and reflect multiple layers of memory about the war and its

FIGURE 9

Confederate Monument, Courthouse Square, Oxford, Mississippi
(1907).

FIGURE 10

Confederate Monument, University of Mississippi, Oxford, Mississippi (1906).

aftermath. On *Confederate Decoration Day, Mrs. Virginia Dupre, Colonel Sartoris's sister, twitched a lanyard and the spring-restive bunting collapsed and flowed, leaving the marble effigy—the stone infantryman on his stone pedestal on the exact spot where forty years ago the Richmond officer and the local Baptist minister had mustered in the Colonel's regiment, and the old men in gray and braided coats . . . tottered into the sunlight and fired shotguns at the bland sky and raised their cracked, quavering voices in the shrill hackle-lifting yelling which Lee and Jackson and Longstreet and the two Johnsons . . . had listened to amid the smoke and the din; epilogue and epitaph, because apparently neither the U.D.C. ladies who instigated and bought the monument, nor the architect who designed it nor the masons who erected it, had noticed that the marble eyes under the shading marble palm stared not toward the north and the enemy, but toward the south, toward (if anything) his own rear . . . the wits said (could say now, with the old war thirty-five years past and you could even joke about it—except the women, the ladies, the unsurrendered, the irreconcilable, who even after another thirty-five years would get up and stalk out of picture houses showing Gone With the Wind).*[2]

Of equal interest to Faulkner was the monument in the cemetery at Ripley, Mississippi, his family's ancestral home, the grave of his great-grandfather, author, soldier, railroad builder—prototype of Colonel Sartoris in Faulkner's third novel: *He stood on a stone pedestal, in his frock coat and bareheaded, one leg slightly advanced and one hand resting lightly on the stone pylon beside him. His head was lifted a little in that gesture of haughty pride which repeated itself generation after generation with a fateful fidelity, his back to the world and his carven eyes gazing out across the valley where his railroad ran and the blue, changeless hills beyond, and beyond that the ramparts of infinity itself* (Fig. 11).[3]

In both the actual and the literary venues of Faulkner's Mississippi landscape, such monuments and public sculptures were designed and reared to commemorate things past. As such, they went beyond the myriad and fascinating details of battles and personalities, which Faulkner absorbed through oral tradition, to the larger realm of historical and metaphysical essences. Indeed, they went beyond the recall of mere events to the meaning and the importance, as the marble inscriptions read, of those who died in "a just and holy cause." Significantly, these memorials appeared on the landscape and in the public consciousness during the very years that young William Faulkner began to grow up and to encounter the myths and realities of the "Lost Cause." As such, they remained, in art and in life, the most consciously contrived examples of the presence of the past in the present.

FIGURE II

Cemetery Statue of Colonel W. C. Falkner (1825–1889), Ripley,
Mississippi.

Three

"OF SECRET AND VIOLENT BLOOD"

The Indian Mounds of Yoknapatawpha

How similar yet how different the family and Confederate memorials were from the funereal monuments on the same landscape of an earlier time and people: the burial mounds of the Chickasaw Indians, who had inhabited the area for centuries. The Spanish explorer Hernando de Soto had found a flourishing Chickasaw civilization when, in 1541, he established his winter camp in the main Chickasaw town of Chicaca in what would become Pontotoc County. In the Treaty of Pontotoc (1832), under great pressure from the United States government and its restless white constituents, the roughly four thousand people of the Chickasaw nation had surrendered their ancestral lands and followed the "Trail of Tears" to the new Indian Territory in what would become Oklahoma. Unlike the neighboring Choctaws in central Mississippi, a third of whom elected to remain on small reservations there, the Chickasaws' removal was virtually complete. Though few, if any, "full-blooded" Chickasaws remained in Mississippi in Faulkner's lifetime, he allowed a few imagined remnants of the group to inhabit his writing.[1]

More lasting, however, in both history and fiction, were the burial mounds of Lafayette, Tippah, and Yoknapatawpha counties, emphatic constructions of bermed earth that would stand through the centuries to remind and rebuke (Figs. 12 and 13). Faulkner knew the several mounds around Oxford, and he owned an illustrated history of Mississippi archaeology that documented their presence throughout the state. In his partially autobiographical essay "Mississippi," he mused on the mounds in which the

FIGURE 12

Indian Mound, Lafayette County, Mississippi (photographed in 1913).

FIGURE 13

Indian Mound, Tippah County, Mississippi (photographed in 1918).

Native Americans *would leave the skulls of their warriors and chiefs and babies and slain bears, and the shards of pots, and hammer- and arrow-heads and now and then a heavy silver Spanish spur.*[2]

In the "Old Man" portion of *The Wild Palms,* in various sections from *Go Down, Moses,* and in numerous short stories, mounds appear as both subject and backdrop, as hauntingly mute but resonant monuments of, and to, their dispossessed builders. In the story "A Bear Hunt," five miles *down the river from Major de Spain's camp, and in an even wilder part of the river's jungle of cane and gum and pin oak, there is an Indian mound. Aboriginal, it rises profoundly and darkly enigmatic, the only elevation of any kind in the wild, flat jungle of river bottom . . .* possessing *inferences of secret and violent blood, of savage and sudden destruction, as though the yells and hatchets which we associated with Indians through the hidden and secret dime novels which we passed among ourselves were but trivial and momentary manifestations of what dark power still dwelled or lurked there, sinister, a little sardonic, like a dark and nameless beast lightly and lazily slumbering with bloody jaws—this, perhaps due to the fact that a remnant of a once powerful clan of the Chickasaw tribe still lived beside it under Government protection.*[3]

As such, the mounds loomed on the landscape like the less hidden structures of the early white settlers—especially their great plain barns. While living among the Indians on the future site of Oxford in 1835, John J. Craig, John Chisholm, and John D. Martin negotiated with the Chickasaws the sale of two sections of land for making a town. As they began selling lots to other settlers, they donated fifty acres of public space that would constitute the square and the lots surrounding it. The county was named in honor of the French-born hero of the American Revolution, the Marquis de Lafayette, and the town, incorporated in 1837, was named for Oxford, the English university seat, in the hopes of attracting the state's primary institution of higher learning. In his fictive name for the town, Faulkner chose to honor another great figure from the Revolutionary era, Thomas Jefferson, but for the fictive county, significantly, he chose the name of an actual river in the southern part of Lafayette County, bearing the Chickasaw Indian name for slashed, or cut-opened land—Yoknapatawpha.[4]

Four

"ALIEN YET INVIOLABLY DURABLE"

The Folk Architecture of Yoknapatawpha

"Folk," "vernacular," "primitive" architecture pervades Faulkner's world, buildings that elude and transcend chronology and that reach from the earliest times into the twentieth century. They are hard, tough structures, symbolic for Faulkner not only of the meanness of life for some, but of the patience and persistence and endurance of the people who built and used them. Originally such buildings were of logs, notched at the corners, a technique similar to that used in various Native American structures. In its European form, log construction was brought across the Atlantic not by the British but by German and Scandinavian immigrants, who settled in the eastern colonies and passed on their log building techniques to English- and African-Americans as settlement pushed west and south in the eighteenth and nineteenth centuries.

"The first houses in new areas of settlement were usually crudely constructed," historian James Latham has noted. "These were temporary, to be used only until something more substantial could be built." There was a great difference between the early, one-room "log cabin," an Irish term, and the more permanent and technically and socially substantial "log house." Spatially, the basic form of the Southern folk house was the so-called single pen, a rectilinear, one-room log structure whose short side averaged some seventeen feet as compared with the long side of approximately twenty feet. It had a gable roof with a single chimney centered along one of the gable ends. Front and back doors were usually centered opposite each other in the two long sides.[1]

FIGURE 14

Dogtrot House, Lafayette County, Mississippi (nineteenth century).

When it became necessary to enlarge such houses, the usual method was to add a similar structure to one of the gable ends. If the addition occurred at the end opposite the chimney, the structure, now composed of two single pens, was logically called a "double pen house," with separate front entrances into the two rooms and a second end chimney in the center of the new gable. If the addition to the single pen was made to the chimney end, the resulting "saddleback house" had a central chimney that served both rooms, while usually retaining the double-pen practice of separate entrances from the porch. Since there were obvious difficulties in adding to notch-cornered log structures, the simplest solution frequently was to connect two single pens by an open passageway, with the passageway and both houses covered by one continuous roof, forming the popular "dogtrot" house (Figs. 14, 15, and 17).[2]

In addition to the technical rationale for constructing them that way, the open breezeway of the dogtrot house was a pleasant place for sitting and socializing, and the type became a ubiquitous building form, not only in the countryside but, in its formative years, of the Southern town as well. It was also referred to as a "dogrun," a "possumtrot," and "two pens and a passage." Like the single and double pen and the

Dogtrot House, Lafayette County, Mississippi (nineteenth century), photograph by Martin Dain.

saddleback house, moreover, it continued as a building type long after notched-log buildings gave way in the middle and later nineteenth century to the so-called "balloon frame," a form and a technique made possible by the new combination of recently invented metal nails, readily planed lumber, and, with the coming of the railroad, easily shipped planks. Sometimes older log structures were covered over and "remodeled" with such boards.

The dogtrot house could also be expanded into much grander forms, with the open passageway enclosed as a front stairhall to a new second floor. Such greatly enlarged houses might then be graced with a two-storey portico across all or part of the front facade, becoming in the process a homegrown version of the neoclassical house. This development characterized the houses of several prominent Oxford families whose histories Faulkner knew. They included the one-storey home, later named "Lindfield," of David Craig (ca. 1837), one of the early settlers of Oxford, a house located two blocks from the larger Shegog House (1848), which Faulkner would purchase in 1930 and live in the rest of his life. A rude, double-pen log house was also the basis of the home of another pioneer, Samuel Carothers, who later enlarged the house into a stately, two-storey dwelling with a six-columned portico across the front. In 1847, Dr. Thomas Dudley Isom, another of the town's earliest settlers, acquired the house and continued to improve and embellish it (Fig. 16).[3] Indeed, the transformation from humble necessity to neoclassical grandeur epitomized the social ascendancy of a number of Faulkner's most vivid fictitious characters.

Still, *un*enlarged folk buildings, inhabited by both black and white Mississippians, were even more familiar structures in Faulkner's world, particularly in the Snopes trilogy. In *The Mansion*, ironically, a dogtrot house lay on *a road marked with many wheels and traced with cotton wisps, yet dirt, not even gravel, since the people who lived on and used it had neither the voting power to compel nor the money to persuade the Beat supervisor to do more than scrape and grade it twice a year. So what he found was . . . what he had expected: a weathered, paintless dog-trot cabin enclosed and backed by a ramshackle of also paintless weathered fences and outhouses—barns, cribs, sheds—on a rise of ground above a creek-bottom cotton patch where he could already see the whole Negro family and perhaps a neighbor or so too dragging the long stained sacks more or less abreast up the parallel rows.* (Fig. 17).[4]

In *The Hamlet*, the first volume of the trilogy, critic Michael Millgate argues, Faulkner's description of Mink Snopes's house is "important for its own sake, as an additional facet of the analytical portrait of the area, but it is also crucial to our understanding of Mink himself and of the reasons why he murders Houston. Thus there is obvious dramatic point in the utter poverty of the place being evoked through the eyes of Mink

FIGURE 16

Carothers-Isom House, Oxford, Mississippi (1843 and later).

himself as he returns from the murder." *It was dusk. He emerged from the bottom and looked up the slope of his meagre and sorry corn and saw it—the paintless two-room cabin with an open hallway between and a lean-to kitchen, which was not his, on which he paid rent but not taxes, paying almost as much rent in one year as the house had cost to build; not old yet the roof of which already leaked . . . just like the one he had been born in, which had not belonged to his father either* (Plates 2 and 3).[5]

Later still, Millgate contends, as Mink is being taken to jail in Jefferson, "his own background is implicitly evoked in terms of his awareness . . . of the trim and prosperous world of Jefferson." The comparison is shattering: *the surrey moving now beneath an ordered overarch of sunshot trees, between the clipped and tended lawns where children shrieked and played in bright small garments in the sunset and the ladies sat rocking in the fresh dresses of afternoon and the men coming home from work turned into the neat painted gates, toward plates of food and cups of coffee in the long beginnings of twilight.* Compared to the environment in which he had spent his life, this world, however enviable, was alien to Mink. It was a milieu he could never imagine entering, though one into which his more resilient cousin, Flem, would cunningly ingratiate himself.[6]

FIGURE 17

Dogtrot House, Lafayette County, Mississippi (nineteenth century).

In *As I Lay Dying,* much the same kind of implicit social and architectural comparison occurred in Addie Bundren's posthumous trip to the Jefferson cemetery from the farm on which she had lived. There a cotton house had been made of *rough logs, from between which the chinking has long fallen. Square, with a broken roof set at a single pitch, it leans in empty and shimmering dilapidation in the sunlight, a single broad window in two opposite walls giving on to the approaches of the path.*[7]

Mildly updated versions of such structures would continue to appear on the out-skirts of Jefferson into the twentieth century, with subtle markings in their main-tenance and accoutrements, demarcating race and class. In *Knight's Gambit,* young Benbow Sartoris, on leave from the Army Air Corps in 1942, observed such houses as he returned by train to Jefferson. He sensed that the train was *beginning to pass the familiar land: the road crossings he knew, the fields and woods where he had hiked as a cub then a scout. . . . Then the shabby purlieus themselves timeless and durable . . . the first Negro cabins weathered and paintless until you realized it was more than just that and that they were a little, just a little awry, not out of plumb so much as beyond plumb: as though created for, seen in or by a different perspective, by a different architect, for a different purpose or anyway with a*

FIGURE 18

African-American working-class houses, Holly Springs, Mississippi (early twentieth century).

*different past . . . each in its fierce yet orderly miniature jungle of vegetable patch . . . and
usually a tethered cow and a few chickens, the whole thing—cabin outpost washpot shed
and well—having a quality flimsy and make-shift, alien yet inviolably durable like Crusoe's
cave; then the houses of white people, no larger than the Negro ones but never cabins, not to their
faces anyway or you'd probably have a fight on your hands, painted or at least once painted, the
main difference being that they wouldn't be quite so clean inside* (Fig. 18).[8]

Yet such dwellings also recall the very beginnings of Jefferson, as described in Faulkner's Compson appendix to *The Portable Faulkner: a solid square mile of virgin North Mississippi dirt as truly angled as the four corners of a cardtable top (forested then because these
were the old days before 1833 when the stars fell and Jefferson, Mississippi was one long rambling
one-storey mudchinked log building housing the Chickasaw agent and his tradingpost store).*[9]

Stores of all varieties were crucial in Faulkner's work: social as well as commercial
structures, places to see and meet other people, to transact business, personal and
professional; important stages in Faulkner's world of comings and goings for the most
rural people whose visits to such places constituted a primitive window on a larger

FIGURE 19

College Hill Store, steps and door, College Hill, Mississippi (late
nineteenth century).

world. The store in the hamlet of College Hill, northwest of Oxford, dated originally from the late nineteenth century and remained unchanged through the mid-twentieth century—except for the modernist intrusion of the red gas pump outside (cover and Fig. 19). The College Hill Store was used by MGM as an important set location in its filming of Faulkner's *Intruder in the Dust*. Descriptions of stores in *Intruder, The Hamlet*, and various stories evoke the penumbral attributes of buildings, especially the smells, much in the manner of Proust's *Remembrance of Things Past*. In "Barn Burning": *The store in which the Justice of the Peace's court was sitting smelled of cheese. The boy, crouched on his nail keg at the back of the crowded room, knew he smelled cheese, and more: from where he sat he could see the ranked shelves close-packed with the solid, squat, dynamic shapes of tin cans whose labels his stomach read.*[10]

Faulkner somehow failed to characterize the oldest, largest, and most important small-town store in north Mississippi, the upscale J. E. Neilson Company, founded in 1839 by one of Oxford's oldest and most prominent families. He seemed to be drawn to its smaller, more rural variants, as typified in such establishments as D. Pointer and Company, in nearby Como, Mississippi (Figs. 22–26). In *The Hamlet*, Faulkner described a store's *now deserted gallery, stained with tobacco and scarred with knives*. The reference to knives may have come from his familiarity with a store in the hamlet of Taylor, Mississippi, south of Oxford, where old men's, possibly absent-minded, pocket-knife whittling had nearly carved away the wooden benches in front (Fig. 20). Faulkner's notable talent for compiling elegant lists reached its apogee in describing the interiors of such stores, as for example in the Compson appendix to *The Portable Faulkner*, where in 1943 the town librarian seeks out Jason Compson to show him a color picture in a glossy magazine of his prodigal sister, Caddy, photographed with a Nazi general staff officer. Here again, in his inimitable way, Faulkner made his point with a coruscating contrast between Caddy's corruptly elegant, high-profile notoriety and the dusty layers of the hometown store where her brother's "office" was housed. In this passage, Faulkner also made the point that there were buildings and spaces in Yoknapatawpha which, if not "gender specific," were at least accepted as male or female domains, the transgression of which had important symbolic connotations of self-assured determination (Figs. 21–26). The librarian *entered the farmer's supply store where Jason IV had started as a clerk and where he now owned his own business as a buyer of and dealer in cotton—striding on through that gloomy cavern which only men ever entered—a cavern cluttered and walled and stalagmite-hung with plows and discs and loops of tracechain and singletrees and mulecollars and sidemeat and cheap shoes and horse linament and flour and molasses . . . and strode on back to Jason's particular domain in the rear, a railed enclosure cluttered with shelves and pigeonholes bearing spiked dust-and-lint-gathering gin receipts and ledgers and cotton samples and rank with the blended smell of cheese and kerosene and harness oil and the tremendous iron stove against which chewed tobacco had been spat for almost a hundred years, and up to the long high sloping counter behind which Jason stood.*[11]

The folk houses and country stores were similar to the larger, if equally primitive, barns, cotton gins, churches, warehouses (Figs. 27 and 28), and train stations (Figs. 29–31, 33) of Yoknapatawpha. Unlike the elegant *Beaux-Arts* terminals in Memphis, Jackson, and even Holly Springs, the simple, utilitarian small-town train stations in Oxford, Ripley, Como, and Batesville were particularly prominent in Faulkner's world. The depot in Oxford (Fig. 29) was a lively nexus of comings and goings for townsmen and University students alike. Especially at the nearby coffee house, "The Shack," which overlooked the station, Faulkner joined fellow students in lively socializing. From the same station in Yoknapatawpha, Quentin Compson departed for Harvard, and countless Jeffersonians entrained for Memphis, New Orleans, and exotic points beyond. More ominously, from the same station in Jefferson, Temple Drake, in *Sanctuary,* began her perilous journey, which darkened even more precipitously as she abandoned the train a few miles south in the station at Taylor.

Compared to the high elegance of the neo-Gothic Episcopal Church in Jefferson, Dilsey's primitive church in *The Sound and the Fury* (Fig. 32) presented a palpably different image: *The road rose again, to a scene like a painted backdrop. Notched into a cut of red clay crowned with oaks the road appeared to stop short off, like a cut ribbon. Beside it a weathered church lifted its crazy steeple like a painted church, and the whole scene was as flat and without perspective as a painted cardboard set upon the ultimate edge of the flat earth, against the windy sunlight of space and April and a midmorning filled with bells. Toward the church they thronged with slow sabbath deliberation. The interior had been decorated, with sparse flowers from kitchen gardens and hedgerows, and with streamers of coloured crepe paper. Above the pulpit hung a battered Christmas bell, the accordion sort that collapses. The pulpit was empty, though the choir was already in place, fanning themselves although it was not warm.*[12]

Indeed, in Yoknapatawpha's folk, vernacular buildings, the actual and the apocryphal were remarkably consanguine.

FIGURE 20

Stores, Taylor, Mississippi (late nineteenth century).

FIGURE 21

Goodwin and Brown's Commissary, Courthouse Square, southeast side, Oxford, Mississippi (1880s).

Counter, D. Pointer & Company, Como, Mississippi (late nineteenth century, demolished).

FIGURE 23

Scales, D. Pointer & Company.

FIGURE 24

Desk, D. Pointer & Company.

FIGURE 25

Snuff Shelf, D. Pointer & Company.

FIGURE 26

Shoes and Cornice, D. Pointer & Company.

FIGURE 27
Warehouses, Back Street, Como, Mississippi (late nineteenth century).

FIGURE 28
Stores and Warehouses, Back street, Como, Mississippi (late nineteenth century).

FIGURE 29

Train Station, Oxford, Mississippi (late nineteenth century).

FIGURE 30

Train Station, Como, Mississippi (late nineteenth century, demolished).

FIGURE 31

Train Station and Coca-Cola sign, Como, Mississippi.

FIGURE 32

Armstead Chapel, C.M.E. Church, Oxford, Mississippi
(mid-twentieth century).

FIGURE 33

Stop Sign, Train Station, Como, Mississippi.

Five

"THE ASPIRATIONS AND THE HOPES"

The Greek Revival of Yoknapatawpha

To his grandest characters, as to Faulkner himself, the most favored architecture was the neoclassical, especially the local variants of the international Greek Revival, the symbol, even in decay, of what Faulkner believed were the better impulses of Southern civilization. The Greek Revival was a romantic, mid-nineteenth-century phenomenon, the latest in a long series of neoclassical movements that had begun with the Italian Renaissance in the fifteenth and sixteenth centuries. The evolution had become more florid in the Baroque and Rococo styles as they moved northward through France, Austria, and the German states in the seventeenth and eighteenth centuries. Britain, and later America, were less touched by the Baroque and Rococo than by the earlier, less encumbered Renaissance modes. The greatest influence on British and American building was, in fact, the work of a single, late Renaissance architect, Andrea Palladio (1508–1580). In his penchant for orthogonal, domed structures, Palladio's models were arcuated Roman variations on trabeated Greek forms, an emphasis that would likewise permeate high-style British and American architecture into the early nineteenth century.

Constitutional government, argues historian Leland Roth, "was an experiment in applied Enlightenment philosophy which rejected monarchical absolutism and attempted to recreate the natural society in which it was believed men were meant to live. Thus architects correspondingly rejected Baroque-Rococo complication of form in search of a simpler architecture suggestive of the first civilized state of primal man." Since the founders of the American Republic, moreover, had "borrowed so heavily from the form and terminology of the Roman republican government, it was natural that Roman architectural forms should be among the first used by American architects." Particularly in the work of Thomas Jefferson and Benjamin Latrobe, and especially in the planning of the new national capital at Washington, an abstract version of Roman forms predominated.[1]

The revival in the mid-nineteenth century of simpler, purer, pre-Roman, Greek architecture was, on the one hand, a logical extension of the Roman Revival and, on the other, a reactive retreat from the Roman leanings of previous generations. It thus brought into sharper relief the affinities and differences between the Greek and Roman architectures of antiquity. In addition to the formal, geometric differences between Greek trabeation and the Roman amalgamation of trabeated and arcuated forms, there were cultural and contextual differences that further contributed to regional preferences for Greek architecture in mid-nineteenth-century America, especially in the rural South. While the general image of Roman building suggested urban juxtapositions, annexations, and collisions of forms, as in the Roman Forum, the chief image of Greek architecture was of serenely discrete structures, related to but interstitially separated from each other, as on the Acropolis in Athens.[2]

Further stimulated by the early-nineteenth-century Greek war of independence from the Turks, the Greek Revival was an international movement that permeated the western world, including all portions of the United States. Indeed, most Americans, north and south, who built or used neoclassical buildings were unbothered by archaeological distinctions between "Greek" and "Roman." Yet, to philosophically inclined Southerners, the appeal of Greek architecture was more than that of just a new aesthetic fashion. The predominantly rural social structure of the American South, the penchant for placing important buildings in relatively serene isolation, helped to contribute to the region's affinity for things Greek. Even in the twentieth century, Faulkner himself would tell a friend that he would *love to go to Greece. All that we learned that's good comes from there.*[3]

Aided by James Stuart and Nicholas Revett's seminal study, *The Antiquities of Athens* (1763), American pattern books, such as Asher Benjamin's illustrated *Practical Home Carpenter* (1830) recorded proportions and details of Greek orders and provided models and instructions that local artisans could develop.[4]

The finest Greek Revival building in Faulkner's Lafayette County was the Lyceum Building (1844–48) on the University of Mississippi campus, with its grandly over-

FIGURE 34

College Church, College Hill, Mississippi (ca. 1844).

scaled portico faced with six huge Ionic columns (Fig. 2). It was designed by the nationally renowned neoclassicist William Nichols (1777–1854), architect of the Mississippi State Capitol (1833 40) and the Mississippi Governor's Mansion (1836– 42), both of which Faulkner would use and analyze in *Requiem for a Nun*. Faulkner admired but never mentioned the Lyceum in his work, probably because, significantly, in the parallel world of Yoknapatawpha the University was placed not in Jefferson but in the nearby town of "Oxford," where in reality it actually resides. This is one of several arguments for the often stated, though still underappreciated, contention that the "prototype" for Jefferson is a composite of several places and is at least partially based on Ripley, located some fifty miles northeast of Oxford, the same distance, approximately, between "Jefferson" and "Oxford."

A small but important Greek Revival building in Faulkner's personal life was the College (Presbyterian) Church (1846), in College Hill, Mississippi, four miles north-west of Oxford, an elegantly simple brick structure with a strong, Doric-columned portico (Fig. 34). After the slave gallery at the rear of the sanctuary was removed, two small, white outside doors remained as traces high up toward the ceiling of the portico facade, hanging as though suspended in space, the outside stairs accessing them having

FIGURE 35

First Lafayette County Courthouse, Oxford, Mississippi (1840; photograph, 1862).

been removed. Though Faulkner never used the church directly in his work, it was the scene in 1929 of his marriage to Estelle Oldham Franklin.

Still, the most significant building in all of Faulkner's work was the county court-house, the symbol, he argued in *Requiem for a Nun*, not only of law and justice, but spiritually, psychologically, architecturally, the center around which life revolves: *the focus, the hub; sitting looming in the center of the county's circumference like a single cloud in its ring of horizon, laying its vast shadow to the uttermost rim of horizon; musing, brooding, symbolic, and ponderable, tall as cloud, solid as rock, dominating all: protector of the weak; judiciate and curb of the passions and lusts, repository and guardian of the aspirations and the hopes; rising course by course during that first summer* (Fig. 35).[5]

Though the name of the original architect has not survived, the Lafayette County Courthouse was built, and possibly designed, by the contractors Gordon and Grayson and was completed on January 12, 1840, at the then-sumptuous cost of $25,100. Faulkner later decided that in Yoknapatawpha, the designer of the building should be the same "French architect" who designed "Sutpen's Hundred," an analogous "grand design" in the private realm. In a crucial passage in *Requiem for a Nun*, Faulkner emphasized that of all the county's buildings, the courthouse *came first, and . . . with stakes and hanks of fishline, the architect laid out in a grove of oaks opposite the tavern and the store, the square and simple foundations, the irrevocable design not only of the courthouse but of the town too, telling them as much: "in fifty years you will be trying to change it in the name of what you will call progress. But you will fail . . . you will never be able to get away from it."* [6]

Faulkner then linked the courthouse to the larger town and county, a strong example of his interest in urban design, an interest perhaps partially engendered by the fact that his maternal great-grandfather, Charles Butler, in the late 1830s surveyed and laid out the town of Oxford. The courthouse was situated in the center of the Square *quadrangular around it, the stores, two-storey, the offices of the lawyers and doctors and dentists, the lodge rooms and auditoriums, above them; school and church and tavern and bank and jail each in its ordered place.* (Fig. 36). Unlike the actual Oxford Square (Fig. 7), which had six roads leading from it—one each from the center of the north and south sides, one each from the four corners—Faulkner devised for the Jefferson Square the more elegant arrangement of four roads leading to and from the exact centers of the four sides of the courthouse: *the four broad diverging avenues straight as plumb-lines in the four directions, becoming the network of roads and by-roads until the whole county would be covered with it.* It was a reification, in the public realm of a frontier Mississippi town, of the ancient idea of the "grand design." [7]

In *Requiem,* in the construction of the fictive building, *eight disjointed marble columns were landed from an Italian ship at New Orleans, into a steamboat up the Mississippi to Vicksburg, and into a smaller steamboat up the Yazoo and Sunflower and Tallahatchie, to Ikkemotubbe's old landing which Sutpen now owned, and thence the twelve miles by oxen into Jefferson: the two identical four-column porticoes, one on the north and one on the south, each with its balcony of wrought-iron New Orleans grillwork, on one of which—the south one—in 1861 Sartoris would stand in the first Confederate uniform the town had ever seen, while in the Square below the Richmond mustering officer enrolled and swore in the regiment which Sartoris as its colonel would take to Virginia . . .* and *when in '63 a United States military force burned the Square and the business district, the courthouse survived. It didn't escape: it simply survived: harder than axes, tougher than fire, more fixed than dynamite; encircled by the tumbled and*

FIGURE 36

Courthouse Square, Oxford, Mississippi (late nineteenth century).

blackened ruins of lesser walls, it still stood, even the topless smoke-stained columns, gutted of course and roofless, but immune, not one hair even out of the Paris architect's almost forgotten plumb, so that all they had to do . . . was put in new floors for the two storeys and a new roof and this time with a cupola with a four-faced clock and a bell to strike the hours and ring alarms; by this time the Square, the banks and the stores and the lawyers' and doctors' and dentists' offices had been restored. The actual postbellum courthouse (Figs. 37 and 94) was designed and built ca. 1870 by the firm of Willis, Sloan, and Trigg, Builders and Architects, who did virtually identical plans for two contemporary courthouses in county seats due north of Oxford: Holly Springs, Mississippi, and Bolivar, Tennessee.[8]

Though Faulkner allowed the Jefferson courthouse to survive the war more intact than did its actual Oxford counterpart, and though Jefferson's Square opened to four streets instead of Oxford's six, the similarity of the two environments, both before and after the war, was an exceptional merger of the actual and the apocryphal.

FIGURE 37

Second Lafayette County Courthouse, Oxford, Mississippi,

Willis, Sloan, and Trigg, architects (ca. 1870).

The greatest quantity of neoclassical buildings, and after the courthouse the largest and finest, was the impressive cluster of Greek Revival houses of the Yoknapatawpha gentry, symbols for Faulkner of a quality of life and a quality of people he admired and emulated despite their personal flaws and despite the flaws of the society that reared them—based upon slavery and a black-white caste system. Just as Jefferson and Yoknapatawpha were amalgamations of several actual Mississippi towns and counties, the homes of Faulkner's characters were composites of actual houses on the north Mississippi landscape.

The most typical regional form of the neoclassical house was a nearly square or rectangular one- or two-storey box with a relatively small four-columned porch on one or more sides. Above the front door, and sometimes a side door, there was usually another door in the second storey leading onto a small balcony. Window shutters, usually painted dark green, were functional screens against sun and weather as well as decorative counterpoints to the standard white walls. Other ornament on the generally chaste buildings might include a wrought-iron railing for the second floor balconies (Plate 6 and Fig. 38). On either side of the central hall lay the parlor, library, dining room, and, in one-storey houses, bedrooms. The central stairhall in two-storey houses led to upstairs bedrooms. In the middle third of the nineteenth century, this mode was especially popular in Mississippi, Alabama, and Tennessee. Oxford and Lafayette County, during Faulkner's lifetime, contained over a dozen extant examples of this type of house, as well as several houses of even grander pretensions, marked by a six- or eight-columned portico extending across the entire front.

The architect-builder in antebellum Oxford most associated with the four-column type was William Turner, a talented though untrained designer who had come to Oxford as a young man sometime around 1840 with his parents, Samuel and Elizabeth Turner, from their home in Iredell County, North Carolina. Turner was the documented designer-builder of several such houses and the possible architect of all or most of the others. If he was not the actual designer for every house of this type, his work could have served as a model for structures by other builders which bore a remarkably close family resemblance. Antebellum houses in this mode in Oxford included the homes of the Craig, Eades, Howry, Shegog, Neilson, Carter, and Thompson families, as well as two successive residences William Turner built for himself. Plantation houses in the four-column mode were built in the county for various owners, including the Price, Wiley, Shipp, and Jones families (Plate 5).[9]

At least five houses, known or believed to have been designed and built by Turner, were imposing edifices on the Oxford townscape. Two of these, the Carter-Tate and

Carter-Tate House, Oxford, Mississippi, attributed to William
Turner, architect (1859).

Neilson-Culley homes, were designed in 1859, with two-storey, four-column porticoes on the front and one side (Fig. 38 and Plate 6). The builder of one of these, Dr. Robert Otway Carter, was the great-great-grandson of the legendary Robert "King" Carter, who in the 1740s, as one of the richest men in Virginia, owned one thousand slaves and three thousand acres of land. Faulkner may have known that "King" Carter allegedly aspired in his grandiose plantation house "Corotoman" to "rival or surpass the Governor's Palace" in Williamsburg, just as Faulkner would later have Thomas Sutpen decree in *Absalom, Absalom!* that "Sutpen's Hundred" should rival or surpass the Yoknapatawpha courthouse. Like the actual Corotoman, Sutpen's Hundred would ultimately succumb to destruction by fire.[10]

It was also Turner who likely designed, for the merchant William S. Neilson, a virtual twin of the Carter house. While the latter passed into the family of the Oxford merchant Henry L. Tate and fell in the twentieth century into picturesque ruin before it was finally razed, the Neilson house in the twentieth century was acquired by the prominent Oxford physician John C. Culley, who with his wife, Nina Somerville Culley, impeccably restored and maintained it. Though Faulkner and Culley had an occasionally strained personal relationship, the two couples were socially amicable, and Faulkner knew the house well, as he knew other buildings by Turner, for example, the house, later named "Cedar Oaks" (1858), that the architect designed for himself on North Lamar Street, two blocks from the Square.[11]

For William Thompson, the brother of the eminent Jacob Thompson, secretary of the interior in President James Buchanan's cabinet, Turner designed his usual two-storey, four-column mansion with the intention that it should replace two smaller, juxtaposed houses, the earliest of which was built ca. 1837 by John D. Martin, one of the founders of Oxford. With the outbreak of war in 1861, only the front half of the new structure had been completed (Figs. 39 and 40). After the war, Thompson's financial condition rendered him incapable of finishing it as planned, and the older, attached structures at the rear were not demolished. Thompson did, however, after United States troops burned the first county courthouse, acquire and surround his house with the wrought-iron fence that had surrounded the courthouse. Faulkner may have known that, like a tree at the Isom Place, north of the Square, the magnolias on the Thompson lawn were brought as seedlings from South Carolina, a symbolic act that Faulkner would later incorporate into his treatment of the Sartoris house.[12]

One of Thompson's daughters, Lucretia, called Lula, married Dr. Josiah Chandler and moved with him and their growing family back into the family home to care for her aging father. In 1893, the last of the Chandler children, Edwin Dial Chandler, was

FIGURE 39

Thompson-Chandler House, Oxford, Mississippi, attributed to William Turner, architect (1860).

FIGURE 40

Thompson-Chandler House.

FIGURE 41

Elma Meek House, Oxford, Mississippi (ca. 1879).

born mentally retarded, a condition known to young William Faulkner. In fact, according to Williams's brother John, the Faulkner boys often noticed Edwin behind the iron fence when they walked by the house. William became upset when neighborhood children taunted Edwin cruelly. Indeed, various observers have surmised that Faulkner based the character Benjy Compson, in *The Sound and the Fury,* on Edwin Chandler. Because of the affinities between the actual and the apocryphal, social and architectural, the Thompson-Chandler house by the mid-twentieth century was often referred to in Oxford as "the Compson house." [13]

The Turner-designed house that Faulkner knew best was one of the architect's earliest Oxford commissions, the Shegog Place (1848), across the Taylor Road from the grand Greek Revival home of Jacob Thompson, which was destroyed by Federal troops in 1864. After their marriage in 1929, the Faulkners lived for two years in an apartment on University Avenue in the handsome postbellum neoclassical home of Elma Meek, the Oxford dowager who suggested the name "Ole Miss" for the university yearbook, a name subsequently applied to the institution itself (Fig. 41). In this house Faulkner wrote *Sanctuary* and several important stories, including "A Rose for Emily." In 1930, with his first substantial royalties, Faulkner purchased the dilapidated

FIGURE 42

Sheegog-Faulkner House, Rowan Oak, Oxford, Mississippi,

William Turner, architect (1848).

FIGURE 43

Avant-Stone House, Oxford, Mississippi (mid-1840s).

Shegog residence and lovingly began to restore it, getting to know the building and the construction process intimately as he worked with the carpenters in its slow resuscitation (Fig. 42). Another nearby structure of the four-column type was the Howry-Wright house on University Avenue, begun ca. 1837, probably as a modest structure that evolved, in the prescribed way, into a neoclassical house. Faulkner may have known, since he would later use the idea in his work, that, as at other houses in the region, Union troops dug up the front lawn in search of silver and other valuables purported to be buried there.[14]

The grandest house in Oxford that Faulkner knew well was the Avant-Stone mansion, built in the early 1840s on the Old College Hill Road near the northwest edge of town by Tomlin Avant, the youngest son of a prosperous Virginia family who had, nonetheless, arrived penniless in Oxford in the late 1830s (Fig. 43). The name of his architect has not survived; if it was William Turner, it was a departure from his usual four-column prototype. Its similarity to several houses in Mississippi and Alabama by the famed William Nichols suggests that the architect of the Lyceum, who spent several years in Oxford in the early and middle 1840s, *could* have been Avant's architect. By building a great house, on borrowed money, Avant hoped to purchase instant status and ultimately prosperity in his adopted community, and he therefore entertained lavishly in his large, white, two-storey residence with its six-columned portico running the entire front length of the house. The impressive doorway from the upstairs hall duplicated the scale of the main, first-floor entrance as it opened onto a shallow, wrought-iron balcony. After Avant went bankrupt, the house went through several owners, including University of Mississippi Chancellor Edward Mayes and his famous father-in-law, senator, presidential cabinet member, and Supreme Court justice, Lucius Quintus Cincinnatus Lamar. By 1892, the house was vacant and in ill repair when the lawyer, James Stone, purchased and restored it. There, his son Phil, Faulkner's closest hometown friend and mentor, grew up as a child and continued to live as an adult, enjoying, among other things, the remnants of the vast library left behind by Mayes and Lamar. It was a house, and a library, that Faulkner knew intimately before it burned to the ground in 1942.[15]

Similar to the four-column Turner-designed homes in town were "Cedar Hill Farm," built ca. 1852 by Yancy Wiley in the northwest quadrant of Lafayette County (Fig. 44), and the Shipp plantation house, located south of Oxford near the southern border of the county (Plate 5 and Fig. 45). Though no documentation exists, both could easily have been designed by Turner. In 1833, Dr. Felix Grundy Shipp had moved from Hinds County in central Mississippi north into the Chickasaw Cession

FIGURE 44

Cedar Hill Farm, Lafayette County, Mississippi (ca. 1852).

near the future town of Water Valley. In 1839, he bought his Lafayette County land at the Pontotoc land auction and built his first residence—an inn on the stagecoach road. But Shipp was ambitious, and in the late 1850s, began to build his large, imposing mansion.[16]

According to historian Charles B. Cramer, Shipp, with the help of his numerous slaves, built his ten-room house facing the stage road, opposite his first residence: "Bricks used in the construction were made in two brick kilns on the place. The cypress shingles used on the roof of the house were dipped in boiling linseed oil to protect them from the harshness of the weather." The shingles lasted seventy-five years before a tin roof was placed over them. The timber frame was joined with sturdy wooden pegs.[17]

Two large rooms lay on either side of the broad central downstairs hall, which ran the depth of the house from the front portico to a porch at the back. An elegantly curved stairway, with carvings by black slave craftsmen, led to the second floor, which

FIGURE 45

Shipp House, Lafayette County, Mississippi (ca. 1857).

contained one huge room above the two first-floor parlors, the former of which was specially designed for meetings of the Masonic Lodge and the Methodist Quarterly Conference. Another upstairs space, called the Medicine Room, resembled a drugstore, with its shelves and cabinets filled with jars and bottles of medicine that Dr. Shipp dispensed to his patients. Plaster walls throughout the house were composed of sand, molasses, horsehair, and other ingredients. A stunning plaster medallion in the front parlor was a replica of one in Andrew Jackson's home, The Hermitage, near Nashville.

The family maintained the property until the death of Dr. Shipp's daughter Martha in the 1920s, after which the house was boarded up and abandoned. The family heirlooms left behind fell prey to vandals and antique hunters as the house slowly decayed. The abandoned stage road that once ran past it became choked with undergrowth and no longer passable, leaving the house isolated deep in the woods. It was a romantic ruin by the time Faulkner would likely have known it, in the 1920s, and possibly found it a suggestive model for the "Old Frenchman Place." Faulkner may or may not have known that the family had originally come from Shipp's Bend, Tennessee. When in 1936 he drew the famous map of his imagined Yoknapatawpha for the flyleaf of *Absalom, Absalom!,* he placed the hamlet of "Frenchman's Bend" and the nearby mansion, the "Old Frenchman Place," in the southeast quadrant of the county, the actual location of the "Old Shipp Place," as it was already coming to be known (Fig. 8).

An important literary model for Faulkner in the use of architecture as setting and symbol was the older Mississippi writer Stark Young (1881–1963), born in Como in Panola County and raised both there and in Lafayette County after his father, a physician, moved to Oxford in 1895. Young was a student and later a professor of drama and literature at the University of Mississippi before completing a distinguished academic career at the University of Texas and Amherst College. Although his fiction has been dismissed by later critics as belonging to the "moonlight and magnolias" school, Young established a lasting reputation as a preeminent drama critic, writing masterful columns for the *New Republic* and the *New York Times*. He had known young William Faulkner through various Oxford connections, particularly their mutual friend Phil Stone. Young helped Faulkner, despite the latter's weak academic credentials, to gain admission to Ole Miss as a special student. He also made it possible for the aspiring young poet to venture north to New York by allowing him to stay for a time in his own apartment and by finding him work in the bookstore of his friend Elizabeth Prall.

FIGURE 46
Tait House, Panola County, Mississippi (1848, demolished).

Faulkner clearly knew Young's Mississippi novels, the characters and settings of which were closely based on references from Panola and Lafayette counties.[18]

The title of Young's first novel, *Heaven Trees* (1926), derived from the name of the plantation house that served as its central venue. "I took the old Tait House for my setting," he recalled of the mansion around which the town of Como would later develop. It was "a fine place that had seven halls and on three sides porches in the Palladian manner with columns" (Fig. 46). Its builder, Young's uncle, Dr. George Tait, "had a diploma from some university to practice medicine, but his plantations had made that unnecessary, and the number of kin and family connections, from whom no fee could be collected, made it futile so that he soon forgot his saddle bags and devoted himself to books and whiskey. The place was haunted with the ghosts of happy elegance and drunken sprees and sorrow, pranks after the school of the frontier, gardens, celebrations, and the whole sarcasm of past time."[19]

Young's second novel, *The Torches Flare* (1928), was set in twentieth-century "Clearwater," a north Mississippi town closely modeled upon Oxford. There, the house called "Friendship," the home of Dr. Dandridge, one of the book's central characters, strongly resembled several Lafayette County houses of the type designed by William Turner. It was in relatively good condition, compared to its once proud, now decaying contemporary, "The Cedars," which Young described as "a square house, gray and weathered." Around it "there were a few cedar trees, but no lot, no garden, and no wall or fence; only a gateway with posts remained" (Fig. 44).[20]

Similar evocations of Southern mansions, in both pristine and declining condition, appeared in Young's later novels, *River House* (1929) and *So Red the Rose* (1934), the latter of which was partially composed while Young was a guest at Cedar Hill Farm, northwest of Oxford on the College Hill Road. Though Young moved much of the action of his last novel from north Mississippi to the Natchez region in southwest Mississippi, attributes of houses from Lafayette and Panola counties permeate it. For example, he used a famous anecdote from Oxford oral tradition in which, during the Civil War, Union soldiers shot and killed a small Negro boy, while the child was hiding in the limbs of a tree on the lawn of the Neilson House. Faulkner knew Young's novels but left no record of his impressions. Though the older writer significantly anticipated him in his use of architecture as a central and defining element, the genius of Faulkner's achievement surpassed in every way the work of Stark Young, including his use of architecture as metaphor.

As one of the settings for Temple Drake's dark adventures in *Sanctuary,* where she is raped with a corncob by the impotent hoodlum Popeye, Faulkner used the Old Frenchman Place to symbolize social, cultural, moral, and spiritual decay: *The house was a gutted ruin rising gaunt and stark out of a grove of unpruned cedar trees. It was a landmark, known as the Old Frenchman place, built before the Civil War; a plantation house set in the middle of a tract of land; of cotton fields and gardens and lawns long since gone back to jungle, which the people of the neighborhood had been pulling down piecemeal for firewood for fifty years or digging with secret and sporadic optimism for the gold which the builder was reputed to have buried somewhere about the place when Grant came through the county on his Vicksburg campaign. . . . The gaunt ruin of the house rose against the sky, above the massed and matted cedars, lightless, desolate, and profound. The road was an eroded scar too deep to be a road and too straight to be a ditch, gutted by winter freshlets and choked with fern and rotted leaves and branches* (Plate 5 and Fig. 45).[21]

In *The Hamlet,* near the turn of the century, Faulkner presented the same abandoned house as being no longer owned or occupied by the descendants of Louis Grenier, the "old Frenchman," but by the backwoods entrepreneur Will Varner, who *owned most of the good land in the country and held mortgages on most of the rest. He owned the store and the cotton gin and the combined grist mill and blacksmith shop in the village* of Frenchman's Bend *and at least once every month during the spring and summer and early fall . . . he would be seen by someone sitting in a home-made chair on the jungle-choked lawn of the Old Frenchman's homesite . . . chewing his tobacco or smoking his cob pipe, with a brusque word for passers cheerful enough but inviting no company, against his background of fallen baronial splendor.* He rationalized this habit only to V. K. Ratliff, the itinerant sewing machine salesman: *I like to sit here. I'm trying to find out what it must have felt like to be the fool that would need all this . . . just to eat and sleep in. . . . But after all, I reckon I'll just keep what there is left of it, just to remind me of my one mistake. This is the only thing I ever bought in my life that I couldn't sell to nobody.*[22]

Will Varner's attitude to the Old Frenchman's Place, which he owned but did not live in, was one of bemused alienation from the original owners' values and intentions. By contrast, the view of another outsider to another grand house that he not only did not inhabit but had never seen the likes of, was vividly presented in the story "Barn Burning." There, through the mind of the abused and terrorized child, Sarty Snopes, Faulkner suggested the power of architecture to astonish, ameliorate, comfort, and delight (Fig. 40): *Presently he could see the grove of oaks and cedars and the other flowering trees and shrubs where the house would be, though not the house yet. They walked beside a fence massed with honeysuckle and Cherokee roses and came to a gate swinging open between two brick pillars, and now, beyond a sweep of drive, he saw the house for the first time and at that instant he forgot his father and the terror and despair both, and even when he remembered his father again . . . the terror and despair did not return. Because, for all the twelve movings, they had sojourned until now in a poor country, a land of small farms and fields and houses, and he had never seen a house like this before.* Hit's big as a courthouse *he thought quietly, with a surge of peace and joy whose reason he could not have thought into words, being too young for that.*[23]

Smaller, one-storey variants of the same Greek Revival graced Lafayette County in both Oxford and the countryside. Near the hamlet of College Hill, the Buford-Heddleston House (1842; Fig. 47) was characterized by crossing central hallways that opened on two sides onto identical four-columned porticoes, a partial, modestly rural version of Andrea Palladio's grand Villa Rotonda, Vicenza, Italy (ca. 1550). A smaller, but similar house in town, "The Magnolias," was built the same year by an early settler, William Smither (Fig. 48). Such houses, Faulkner wrote in *Knight's Gambit*, were *more spartan even than comfortable even in those days when people wanted, needed comfort in their homes for the reason that they spent* some *of their time there.*[24]

The house that so moved Sarty Snopes in "Barn Burning" was the ancestral seat of the de Spain family, but it could as easily have been the nearby country house "Sartoris," which Faulkner placed in the northwest quadrant of his Yoknapatawpha map, near the actual location of Cedar Hill Farm. It was significant that the Sartoris house

FIGURE 47

Buford-Heddleston House, College Hill, Mississippi (ca. 1842).

FIGURE 48

The Magnolias, Oxford, Mississippi (ca. 1842).

had no made-up name like "Longwood" or "Bellevue" but only the name of the family itself, a name Faulkner saw as having both dark and grand connotations: *For there is death in the sound of it and a glamorous fatality, like silver pennons downrushing at sunset or a dying fall of horns along the road to Rouncevaux.*[25]

In the 1920s, Bayard Sartoris returned to and pondered the meaning of his ancestral home, burned by Federal troops during the Civil War and rebuilt over the original cellar and foundations afterward. Faulkner used such architectural layering to evoke the even more complex layering of the Sartoris family and indeed of Southern history. Though in most of his later work he would emphasize the exteriors of buildings as sculptural monuments on the natural landscape, in *Sartoris* he developed a sense of the layering of interior spaces as well (Fig. 49). It was remarkable that here in the first of his Yoknapatawpha novels, he had already developed a sophisticated sense of architectural symbolism: *Then the road approached the railroad and crossed it and at last the house John Sartoris had built stood among locusts and oaks and Simon* [the driver] *swung between iron gates and into a curving drive. . . . Bayard stood for awhile before his house. The white simplicity of it dreamed unbroken among ancient sunshot trees.* He then crossed the colonnaded veranda and entered the front hall. *The stairway with its white spindles and red carpet mounted in a tall slender curve into upper gloom. From the center of the ceiling hung a chandelier of crystal prisms and shades, fitted originally for candles but since wired for electricity. To the right of the entrance, beside folding doors rolled back upon a dim room emanating an atmosphere of solemn and seldom violated stateliness and known as the parlor, stood a tall mirror filled with grave obscurity like a still pool of evening water.*

Bayard then climbed the stairs and *stopped again in the upper hall. The western windows were closed with lattice blinds, through which sunlight seeped in yellow dissolving bars that but served to increase the gloom. At the opposite end a tall door opened upon a shallow grilled balcony which offered the valley and the cradling semicircle of the eastern hills in panorama. On either side of this door was a narrow window set with leaded panes of vari-colored glass* which John Sartoris's *younger sister had brought from Carolina in a straw-filled hamper in '69.*[26]

The building, the decay, and sometimes the destruction of such houses were crucial to the plots, the ambience, and the delineation of character in Faulkner's work: from the Old Frenchman Place in *Sanctuary* and *The Hamlet* to similar homes in town of the Compson and de Spain families, to the plantation house, Sutpen's Hundred, in *Absalom, Absalom!* Though such apocryphal grandiosity had no real equivalent on the actual Mississippi landscape, except perhaps at the Tait House in Panola County (1848; Fig. 46), "Waverly" in Clay County (1850; Fig. 49), or houses in the Natchez district, such as

FIGURE 49

Reflected Interiors, Waverly, Clay County, Mississippi, attributed
to Charles Pond, architect (ca. 1850).

"Windsor" in Claiborne County (1860; Figs. 50 and 51), *Absalom, Absalom!* would have lost much of its power without the prominence and the grandeur Faulkner gave to Sutpen's house, the other Grand Design, the private, monomaniacal counterpart of the public Grand Design of courthouse, square, and town. It was the symbol for Thomas Sutpen of the security he craved and worked for, a status denied him earlier at another grand house when he had been asked by a haughty servant to go around to the back door. In the middle of what the elder Jason Compson called *a shadowy miasmic region something like the bitter purlieus of Styx,* Sutpen decreed his own house into being as a kind of commandment: *Be Sutpen's Hundred, like the oldtime "Be Light."* In *Requiem for a Nun,* Faulkner represented the mansion as being *something like a wing of Versailles glimpsed in a Lilliput's gothic nightmare.*[27]

The contrast between the names of the houses on the Sutpen and Sartoris plantations has been noted insightfully by critic William Ruzicka: "Sartoris itself is named, of course, for the family, and the name, in its own way, is an attribute or quality. Sutpen's Hundred is named for the number of square miles it contains—a quantity. The complete name is composed of two words: the possessive form of the owner's name and the quantitative measurement of what is possessed."[28]

The size of the house was, in fact, so colossal that the curious Jefferson gentry, eager to observe the phenomenon, *would make up parties to meet at the Holston House and go out horseback, often carrying lunch. . . . Without dismounting (usually Sutpen did not even greet them with as much as a nod, apparently as unaware of their presence as if they had been idle shades) they would sit in a curious quiet clump as though for mutual protection and watch his mansion rise, carried plank by plank and brick by brick out of the swamp where the clay and timber waited—the bearded white man and the twenty black ones and all stark naked.* Like his slaves, Sutpen worked in the nude, they surmised, because he was *saving his clothes, since decorum even if not elegance of appearance would be the only weapon (or rather, ladder) with which he could conduct the last assault upon . . . respectability.*[29]

Sutpen and his crew of naked slaves *worked from sunup to sundown . . . and the architect in his formal coat and his Paris hat and his expression of grim and embittered amazement lurked about the environs of the scene with his air something between a casual and disinterested spectator and a condemned and conscientious ghost—amazement, General Compson said, not at the others and what they were doing so much as at himself, at the inexplicable and incredible fact of his own presence. But he was a good architect . . . And not only an architect, as General Compson said, but an artist since only an artist could have borne those two years in order to build a house which he doubtless not only expected but firmly intended never to see again. Not, General Compson said, the hardship to sense and the outrage to sensibility of the two years' sojourn, but Sutpen:*

FIGURE 50

Above: Windsor, Claiborne County, Mississippi (1860, burned 1890).

FIGURE 51

Opposite: Windsor, detail.

FIGURE 52

Estes House, Panola County, Mississippi (ca. 1855, demolished).

that only an artist could have borne Sutpen's ruthlessness and hurry and still manage to curb the dream of grim and castlelike magnificence at which Sutpen obviously aimed, since the place as Sutpen planned it would have been almost as large as Jefferson itself was at the time.[30]

Then, when it became altogether too claustrophobic, too threatening, the "French architect"—as much in thrall to Sutpen as were the African slaves he supervised—attempted to escape from it all through the swamp back to the river and south to New Orleans. And in relating this surreal episode, the great Faulkner wit emerges in a novel that is not usually thought to contain much humor, as he turned the word "architect" from a noun into a verb: *It was late afternoon before they caught him . . . and then only because he had hurt his leg trying to architect himself across the river.*[31]

When the work was completed, Sutpen's *presence alone compelled that house to accept and retain human life; as though houses actually possess a sentience, a personality and character acquired, not so much from the people who breathe or have breathed in them inherent in the wood and brick or begotten upon the wood and brick by the man or men who conceived and built them* but rather *in this house an incontrovertible affirmation for emptiness, desertion; an insurmountable resistance to occupancy save when sanctioned and protected by the ruthless and the strong.*[32]

FIGURE 53

Estes House, stairhall.

After surviving the war but not the collisions of Sutpen and his heirs, Sutpen's Hundred, before its ultimate destruction by fire, suffered a decline more ruinous and symbolic even than that of the Old Frenchman Place: *Rotting portico and scaling walls, it stood . . . not invaded, marked by no bullet nor soldier's iron heel, but rather as though reserved for something more: some desolation more profound than ruin . . . that barren hall with its naked stair . . . rising into the dim upper hallway, where an echo spoke which was not mine, but rather that of the lost, irrevocable might-have-been which haunts all houses* (Figs. 52 and 53).[33]

The fall of the House of Sutpen was a nineteenth-century Mississippi version of the fall of the House of Atreus in the Greek dramas of Aeschylus in the fifth century B.C. Indeed, the Greek Revival architecture of Yoknapatawpha was the perfect setting for Faulkner's Greek tragedies.

Six

"IMMOLATED STICKS AND STONES"

The Gothic Revival and Its Kindred Modes

If "Greek tragedy" can be defined as a dramatic or literary composition "with a serious or somber theme," typically of a person whose character is flawed by one or more major weaknesses such as pride, envy, or an overweening ambition "which lead inevitably to his downfall," *Absalom, Absalom!* is certainly in that realm. Yet that novel, like much of Faulkner's work, also has elements of the genre of literature known as the Gothic Novel, "characterized by a gloomy setting, grotesque or violent events and an atmosphere of degeneration and decay." Malcolm Cowley believed that *Absalom* belonged primarily to the latter mode, with Sutpen's Hundred taking the place of "the haunted castle on the Rhine."[1]

Likewise, the Greek and Gothic revivals in nineteenth-century architecture, whatever their differences and distinctions, had many affinities as well. While Greek Revival architecture was in one sense only the latest in a long series of neoclassical movements, it was also a romantic nineteenth-century revolt against the Renaissance and the subsequent centuries of commitments to the neo-Roman. It was thus a deeply consanguine cousin of the Gothic Revival, which had itself begun in the eighteenth century as a revolt against the reasoned order of classicism and had found a sympathetic model in the pointed arches, ribbed vaults, and flying buttresses of the medieval Gothic. Indeed in the pre-Renaissance Gothic and the pre-Roman Greek, nineteenth-century American romantics, particularly in the South, found comfort not only in "yesterday," but in the "days before yesterday."

Both revivals were an integral part of the "romantic" worldview, with its emphasis on the imagination and the emotions, an interest in the remote, and a predilection for melancholy. Given this state of mind, romanticism encouraged not only the revival of the Gothic, but frequently the design of anything remote and exotic, including the "Italian villa" and varieties of "orientalism." Furthermore, this interest in "irregularity" and picturesque asymmetry broke with the orthogonal rectilinearity of neoclassical forms and floor plans and planted the germ that would flourish in the twentieth century into what Frank Lloyd Wright would call "organic" architecture, an architecture that "grew" from the inside out to express its functional, aesthetic, and symbolic needs.

It was fitting that the neo-Gothic, like the medieval Gothic before it, should find its most convincing expression in church architecture and particularly, in the United States, in the work of Richard Upjohn (1802–1878). An Englishman who emigrated to America in 1829, Upjohn insisted that he was "an Episcopalian who happened to be an architect, rather than the reverse." With a great concern for reviving both the essence and the details of medieval English Gothic architecture, he was the major American advocate for the British organization that worked to promote those ends, the Cambridge Camden Society, and its publication, *The Ecclesiologist.*[2]

Upjohn's most famous building was Trinity Church, New York (1846), but he designed dozens of exemplary smaller churches throughout the Northeast. His message, furthermore, was sent to all parts of the country, including Mississippi, via the publication of his "ecclesiological" designs in *Upjohn's Rural Architecture* (1852). Yet Oxford, Mississippi, was the site of a structure, St. Peter's Episcopal Church (ca. 1855–60), not just based on a design from Upjohn's pattern book, but a building most certainly designed by Upjohn himself (Plate 7, Figs. 54 and 55). The circumstantial evidence is the church's complete affinity with Upjohn's ecclesiological style, while documentary proof is limited to a handwritten contemporary note on the back of the church deed, attributing the design to him.[3]

Upjohn was known to Frederick A.P. Barnard, another ardent Episcopalian, who had come from New England and had studied and later taught at Yale in mathematics, chemistry, astronomy, and related sciences. After teaching for sixteen years at the University of Alabama, he moved in 1854 to join the faculty of the University of Mississippi, where in 1859 he became chancellor. In 1861, opposing secession, he returned to New York, where from 1864 to 1889 he served as president of Columbia University. In the late 1850s, he also served as rector of St. Peter's and would have been instrumental in commissioning Upjohn, whom he had known of over the years

FIGURE 54

St. Peter's Episcopal Church, Oxford, Mississippi, attributed to
Richard Upjohn, architect (1859).

FIGURE 55

St. Peter's Episcopal Church, interior.

through their mutual interests in Episcopalian ecclesiology. While the stunningly carved, subtly lit sanctuary was finished ca. 1860, the imposing steeple was not completed until 1893, a gift of the Pegues family. St. Peter's was the church of many prominent Oxonians, including the writer Augustus Baldwin Longstreet and, in the twentieth century, the family of William Faulkner.[4]

Though in *Absalom, Absalom!* Faulkner placed the wedding of Ellen Coldfield and Thomas Sutpen not in St. Peter's, but in the nearby Methodist Episcopal Church, his evocation of the event applied to all British-derived Mississippi denominations. In his depiction, he came close to proposing an ethnocentric interpretation of the importance of architecture: *The crowd outside was quiet yet, perhaps out of respect for the church, out of that aptitude and eagerness of the Anglo-Saxon for complete mystical acceptance of immolated sticks and stones.*[5]

In *Knight's Gambit,* St. Peters's was a significant landmark on the Jefferson landscape for young Benbow Sartoris, returning by train in 1942 for a visit to Jefferson, on leave from the Army Air Corps: *Then he was home: a paved street crossing not very far from the house he had been born in, and now he could see above the trees the water tank and the gold cross on the spire of the Episcopal Church . . . his face pressed to the grimy glass as if he were eight years old.*[6]

Later, in *The Town,* the building, again slightly older than Oxford's St. Peter's, had become a tourist attraction: *There is a small Episcopal church in Jefferson, the oldest extant building in town (it was built by slaves and called the best, the finest . . . by the northern tourists who passed through Jefferson now with cameras, expecting—we don't know why since they themselves had burned it and blown it up with dynamite in 1863—to find Jefferson much older or anyway older looking than it is and faulting us a little because it isn't).*[7] Perhaps this was, on Faulkner's part, a recognition and a premonition of the fame and the tourists that Oxford had acquired, and would acquire, largely because he had immortalized it in his work.

In the mid-nineteenth-century revival of the Gothic and its kindred modes, the greatest theorists and practitioners of such persuasions in residential architecture were two men with similar names, Andrew Jackson Downing (1815–1852) and Alexander Jackson Davis (1803–1892). In his widely influential books, particularly *Cottage Residences* (1842) and *The Architecture of Country Houses* (1850), Downing stressed the relationship of structure and landscape, the latter meant to meander about and toward the building so as to make both seem to be "natural" elements of an integrated composition. Downing was clearly partial to the Gothic: "There is something wonderfully captivating," he wrote, "in the idea of a battlemented castle, even to an apparently modest man, who thus shows to the world his unsuspecting vein of personal ambition." But since the castellated Gothic style never seemed "completely at home except in wild and romantic scenery," he advocated a more domesticated version, the "Tudor," and for those even more modestly situated, he recommended the "rural Gothic," which while "never misplaced in spirited rural scenery, gives character and picturesque expression to many landscapes entirely devoid of that quality." Downing's books were illustrated with designs of his own and of other selected architects, his undoubted favorite among the latter being A. J. Davis, who designed in both grand and modest versions of the popular modes of the day, including the Greek Revival.[8]

The most typical and popular image of the neo-Gothic "Downing-Davis house," as it came to be known, was the compact, two-storey residence, usually with a one-storey veranda across the front and a steeply-pitched roof, the long side of which was punctuated with a prominent central gable or with several large gablelike dormers, all richly trimmed with wooden, gingerbread ornament (Plate 8, Figs. 56 and 57). Though there were, surprisingly, no major manifestations of the type in Oxford itself, there were several impressive examples in Columbus and even closer in Holly Springs, approximately thirty miles to the north, a town in which Faulkner had early social connections and which he knew as well as he knew any Mississippi town next to Oxford and Ripley.

Particularly prominent there were the Gothic Revival homes of the Coxe family, "Airliewood," and the Bonner family, "Cedarhurst," both completed in the late 1850s. Cedarhurst was the home of the writer, Sherwood Bonner, who also served as the personal secretary of Henry Wadsworth Longfellow and hence lived in both Holly Springs and Cambridge (Fig. 57). The house's prominence as a type led historian Leland Roth to cite it in his discussion of the Downing-Davis legacy in his *Concise History of American Architecture*. Since the Bonners built Cedarhurst relatively close to the street, the more spaciously sited Airliewood (Plate 8) is a clearer illustration of the type Faulkner used as the Benbow house in *Sartoris: From the gate, the cinder-packed drive rose in a grave curve between cedars . . . set out by an English architect of the '40s who had built the house (with the minor concession of a veranda) in the funereal light Tudor which the young Victoria had sanctioned* and around which *even on the brightest days lay a resinous exhilerating gloom. . . . It was trimmed with white and it had mullioned casements brought out from England.*[9]

FIGURE 56

Episcopal Rectory, Columbus, Mississippi (ca. 1875). Birthplace of Tennessee Williams.

FIGURE 57

Cedarhurst, Bonner-Belk House, Holly Springs, Mississippi (1858).

FIGURE 58

Walter Place, Holly Springs, Mississippi (1855).

In Mississippi, and throughout America, certain buildings *combined* the neoclassical with the neo-Gothic. Some of these were deliberately composed that way, such as the large and unusual Walter Place in Holly Springs, with its parapeted Gothic towers flanking a Corinthian-columned, Greek Revival center (Fig. 58). Other houses reflecting both styles were more often postbellum, Gothicized remodelings of antebellum, neoclassical structures or at least were buildings to which Victorian gingerbread scrollwork had been added to columns and porches. Examples of the latter included the Simon Spight and Chesley Hines houses in Ripley (Figs. 98 and 99) and the Oxford homes of the Isom and the Kennedy-Price-Shaw families, as well the one-storey house that Faulkner lived in as a child after his family moved to Oxford (Fig. 1). The Freedonia Church in neighboring Panola County, important in the life and work of Stark Young, combined a trabeated, neoclassical portico with pointed, neo-Gothic fenestration (Figs. 59 and 60). Like the Greek Revival Presbyterian Church in College Hill, it contained a separate entrance to the slave balcony at the rear of the sanctuary.

The grandest antebellum house in Oxford that was neither neoclassical nor neo-Gothic was the "Italianate" mansion designed in 1859 for the Pegues family by the

FIGURE 59

Freedonia Church, Panola County, Mississippi, John Scott
McGehee, architect (ca. 1848).

FIGURE 60
Freedonia Church, interior.

acclaimed architect Calvert Vaux (1824–1895) (Plate 9 and Figs. 61–64). Born and educated in England, Vaux emigrated to the United States in 1850 at the behest of none other than Andrew Jackson Downing, who invited him to become his partner, chiefly in the designing of the grounds and buildings of Hudson River estates in the English pastoral manner. After Downing's accidental and untimely death in 1852, Vaux worked with a number of partners, the most eminent of whom was the landscape architect Frederick Law Olmsted, with whom, in the late 1850s, he designed Central Park in New York. Then and later, he designed numerous houses, the plans and renderings of which he published, through five editions, in his widely influential *Villas and Cottages* (1857–74). His public commissions in the late 1870s would include New York's Museum of Natural History and Metropolitan Museum of Art.

Vaux's English ancestors had anglicized, as "Vox," the pronunciation of their originally French name, which Faulkner must have known and assumed was pronounced "Voe." Hence a possible explanation of his fascination with a "French architect," who appears in work after work from *Absalom* to *Sanctuary* to *The Hamlet* and *Requiem for a Nun*. Vaux's Pegues house in Oxford was not merely copied from his pattern book, *Villas and Cottages,* but was built from original drawings signed by the architect

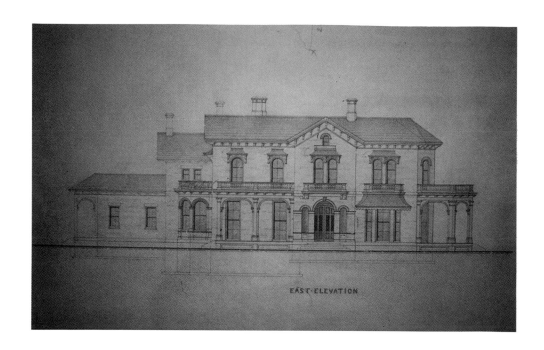

FIGURE 61

Pegues House, Oxford, Mississippi, original elevation signed by
Calvert Vaux, architect (1859).

FIGURE 62

Pegues House, Oxford, Mississippi, Calvert Vaux, architect
(1859).

(Fig. 61). If St. Peter's was attributed on reasonably good evidence to Upjohn, the Pegues house was assuredly designed by Vaux. Though Faulkner never literally described such a house in his work, he felt its presence in more indirect ways.

Thomas Pegues was descended from a prominent South Carolina Huguenot family and, with several brothers, moved through Alabama in the 1840s and settled east of Oxford near the community of Woodson's Ridge. In the early 1850s, he became quite prosperous, eventually owning 4,000 acres and 150 slaves. Then in the late 1850s, with a wife and growing family, he moved to Oxford and started to build his house. Pegues was active in the affairs of St. Peter's Episcopal Church, the most socially prominent congregation in town, as well as of the new University of Mississippi, of which he was a trustee, and it was probably through those activities, perhaps through F. A. P. Barnard's New York connections, that he learned of Vaux and Olmsted and engaged Calvert Vaux to design his house. The Italian style, argued Andrew Jackson Downing, Vaux's first partner, "addresses itself more to the feelings and the senses, and less to the reason or judgment, than the Grecian style, and . . . it is far better suited to symbolize the variety of refined culture and accomplishment which belongs to modern civilization than almost any other style."[10]

The mansion was constructed of brick, molded by black slave craftsmen in kilns on the property (Plate 9, Fig. 62). Specially rounded bricks were devised for the curving bay window on the north side of the house. The round-arched main entrance echoes the shapes of the second floor windows, all topped by elaborate cornices supported by prominent brackets like those defining the roof eaves above them. Through then-novel sliding doors, the central grand stairhall opens north to double parlors and a small library; south, to the dining room and a "winter garden" conservatory (Figs. 63 and 64). Beyond this, the large kitchen with its huge fireplace is integral to the house, unlike the detached kitchen common to most neoclassical homes. No expense, apparently, was spared in the construction of this elegant villa, the full completion of which was delayed until after the Civil War. The careful and talented contractor was none other than William Turner, the designer and builder of much of neoclassical Oxford. In 1864, when much of the town was burned, Union soldiers marched up the driveway and set fire to the house, but when hearing of the imminent approach of Confederate troops, retreated before carrying their task to completion. Family members extinguished the blaze, and one of the South's most significant houses was saved.[11]

In both the actual and the fictional landscapes of north Mississippi, the neo-Gothic and the Italianate modes were second only to the neoclassical in the power of their impact.

FIGURE 63

Pegues House, double parlors.

FIGURE 64

Pegues House, front porch.

Seven

"A KIND OF MAJESTY"

The Postbellum Architecture of Victorian Yoknapatawpha

✣

Following the Civil War, most of the antebellum architectural styles continued to be built sporadically on into the twentieth century, but there was at the same time a marked change of mood. In the South, for a while, there was a poverty-stricken aura of defeatism, inaction, and decay. In the booming, industrial North, there was, by contrast, a new sense of energy, prosperity, posturing, and self-indulgence. Sociologist Thorstein Veblen embalmed the zeitgeist with his memorable phrase "conspicuous consumption." Historian Vernon Louis Parrington stressed another aspect of the era's spirit by calling it "the Great Barbecue." Eventually the "New South," following Reconstruction, would struggle wanly onto the national bandwagon, whistling bravely and building with strained exuberance.

The fashionable "new" architecture of the postwar period was a much encumbered extension of the two major antebellum styles—the neoclassical and the neo-Gothic. The expression of the former, developed largely in France, was a highly strung revival of the seventeenth-century French Baroque, with its mansard roofs and rounded, oval, and curving forms, a revival that was patronized by Emperor Napoleon III and his architect, Baron Georges Haussmann. In the 1860s, 1870s, and 1880s, much of Paris was rebuilt in this style atop a newly reopened city of grand diagonal avenues that were superimposed upon what remained of the meandering medieval streetscape. Because of the "imperial" patronage, the style was called "Second Empire" or, more informally, "Mansardic." The most prominent Second Empire buildings in America were

Alfred B. Mullett's State, War, and Navy Building (1871–75), conspicuously sited just west of the White House; Smithmeyer and Pelz's Library of Congress (1886–97), conspicuously nestled just east of the Capitol; and John McArthur's Philadelphia City Hall, conspicuously monopolizing the central square of William Penn's sternly orthogonal city plan of 1681.

The other side of the postbellum architectural coin was the High Victorian Gothic, made especially popular in the mid-century English architecture of William Butterfield. As opposed to the monochromatic, rounded, mansardic flourishes of the Second Empire, the High Victorian Gothic emphasized pointed, spiky, polychromatic, attenuated versions of Downing and Upjohn's relatively gentle antebellum Gothic Revival. In the north, the most revered and noticed version of this inspired concoction was Ware and Van Brunt's Memorial Hall at Harvard (1871–88), a monument to the Harvard men who had perished for the Union in the Civil War. The Harvard men who had died for the Confederacy received no mention in Ware and Van Brunt's monument. The English savant, John Ruskin, called it the finest building in America. In addition to the two dominant styles, moreover, was a third category of even more exotic variations on, or combinations of, the Mansardic and the High Victorian. This latter potpourri, usually defying classification, was summed up by the phrase: "Too much is not enough."

A relatively pure Oxford example of the Second Empire Mansardic was the Roberts-Neilson House (ca. 1870), conspicuously sited on the town's elegant South Lamar Street (Fig. 65). Above its generous, one-storey front portico ran the handsomely polychromed and densely dormered Mansard roof. A Swedish immigrant designer/craftsman, G. M. Torgerson (1840–1902), who worked on numerous postbellum Oxford buildings, designed the house in the chic new style for the merchant Charles Roberts, who passed the house on to his daughter as he himself acquired the Pegues house and named it "Edgecombe." One door south of the Roberts House rose the kindred Stowers-Longest House (ca. 1895; Fig. 66), a hybrid combination of Victorian modes that imbibed strong doses of the spiky, blocky Eastlake style, an ambience evoked by the English architect Charles Eastlake in his *Hints on Household Taste* (1868), popularized in an American edition of 1872.[1]

A spirited amalgam of Victorian styles coalesced in the splendid and sprightly High Victorian Gothic house for the banker W. L. Archibald on University Avenue at Fifth Street (ca. 1876), with rich interior detailing by Torgerson, who may have designed the entire structure. Later acquired by businessman Peyton Skipwith, the house became for the next half century the domain of his daughter, the redoubtable Kate Skipwith. Blithely demolished by the University in 1974, two years short of its centen-

FIGURE 65

Roberts-Neilson House, Oxford, Mississippi, attributed to G. M.
Torgerson, architect (ca. 1870).

FIGURE 66

Stowers-Longest House (Roberts-Neilson House in background),
Oxford, Mississippi (ca. 1895).

FIGURE 67

Smith House, Holly Springs, Mississippi (ca. 1900).

nial, it was a reigning presence on the Oxford landscape throughout William Faulkner's life. The style continued to appear through the turn of the century, as in the Smith House, Holly Springs (ca. 1900), an exuberant wedding cake of a structure, which in its well-maintained vigor would become more appreciated as its years increased (Fig. 67).[2]

A more sedate version of the style, in Como, Mississippi, had a particularly poignant and ironic history. In 1893, Obedience Pointer Taylor, wife of the planter and cotton broker Robert Taylor, inherited the fabled "Heaven Trees" house of her grandfather, Dr. George Tait (Fig. 46). By the 1890s, the triple-porticoed house, immortalized in Stark Young's fiction, was in bad repair and, besides, was not to Bedie Taylor's taste. She felt no call to preserve the antebellum architecture that had preceded the "Lost Cause." She considered herself a modern woman and therefore wanted what by 1890s standards could be considered a modern house. For this she turned to the best local architect, Anders Johnssen, who, like G. M. Torgerson of Oxford, was a Swedish immigrant and an accomplished designer-craftsman. With innocent good intentions, he had anglicized his name to Andrew Johnson, a moniker that could not have been a popular one in postbellum Mississippi. Nevertheless, he had built a series of stunning residences, churches, and public structures throughout Panola County.

Since the new house for Bedie and Robert Taylor would be placed relatively close to the major street in the booming village of Como, it would not actually threaten the older Tait house, which sat farther back on the property. But there seemed no need to keep them both, and Mrs. Taylor ordered the house of her ancestor demolished. The workmen who were hired to accomplish this, however, reminded her that the lumber from the Tait house was far too rare and fine to be discarded and that it would be both frugal and appropriate to use it in the construction of the new house. Hence the materials of the old Tait mansion were literally transplanted in 1893 to the Victorian Taylor house (Fig. 68). In the early 1940s, the youngest Taylor son married and built a sturdy brick house next door, while his two bachelor brothers lived until their deaths in the decaying Taylor House with its—by now also decaying—"Heaven Trees" lumber. In the 1970s, as the work of its architect, Andrew Johnson, became better appreciated, the house was placed on the National Register of Historic Places and was subsequently restored. Though Faulkner most likely knew little, if any, of this story, it was a social and architectural saga worthy of his richest imaginings.[3]

An equally prominent remodeled Oxford structure that Faulkner knew through family connections was the residence known as "Memory House," the home of his brother John Faulkner. Though first built as a two-storey neoclassical mansion in the

FIGURE 68

Robert Taylor House, Como, Mississippi, Andrew Johnson, architect (1893).

FIGURE 69

Memory House, home of John W. T. Faulkner III, Oxford, Mississippi (ca. 1855 and later).

1850s by the planter Paul Barringer, it passed through several owners in the mid-nineteenth century, including Judge Duke Kimbrough, who in the 1880s removed the Greek Revival portico and replaced it with a Victorian facade complete with a central tower (Fig. 69). In the early twentieth century, J. O. Ramey acquired the house, after which time his daughter, Lucille, infused it with a lively social life. W. C. Handy came down from Memphis to perform at dances there. In 1924, Lucille Ramey married John Fa[u]lkner, who, with their sons Jimmy and Chooky, would endow Memory House with warmth and activity.[4]

The ecclesiastical counterpart of such residential eclecticism was Oxford's hand-some, brick First Presbyterian Church (1881), built on the site of the original frame structure, which had been reared in 1843. In 1864 Union troops torched the building, but an alert church member who lived nearby was able to extinguish the blaze. In the 1870s disagreement developed among differing factions in the congregation as to whether to renovate the old structure or construct a new one. The latter sentiment prevailed, and the new church was dedicated in 1881 (Fig. 70). No record survives to identify the designer or builder, though circumstantial evidence suggests that it could have been G. M. Torgerson, whose architectural presence in Victorian Oxford was comparable to the antebellum hegemony of William Turner's neoclassicism.[5]

The First Presbyterian was a rival to the nearby Cumberland Presbyterian Church, an antebellum neoclassical structure that was itself transformed in the 1880s by a neo-Gothic remodeling. In the First Presbyterian, twin towers of ambiguous stylistic origins flank the central tower and doorway, which leads into the austerely moving interior, a determinedly plain space in contrast to the exterior, embellished only by brilliant stained glass windows set within rounded, neo-Romanesque frames. Members of the congregation included Lemuel and Lida Oldham, the parents of Estelle Oldham Faulkner. The church was thus a structure that would have entered Faulkner's consciousness, not only as a prominent feature on the Oxford landscape, but as a building with personal, familial associations as well.

Another High Victorian building of the vaguely defined "Queen Anne" mode was the new University of Mississippi Library (1889), located on University Circle just north of the Confederate Monument (Fig. 71). An important building in Faulkner's intellectual development, he visited it often, especially as a youth when his family lived in a similar, late-Victorian campus residence nearby. Later, in the early 1920s, after the building had become the home of the Law School, young William Faulkner, pursuing odd jobs, traversed the structure as a part-time carpenter and painter. Still, the most imposing Victorian public building in Faulkner's Oxford was the Federal Court-

FIGURE 70

First Presbyterian Church, Oxford, Mississippi (1881).

house on the northeast corner of the Square (Plate 10). It was built in 1885 in the pervasively popular style of Richardsonian Romanesque, named after the Louisiana-born Boston master H. H. Richardson, whose strong, well-proportioned, free renderings of the medieval Romanesque caught the nation's attention in such monuments as Trinity Church, Boston (1872–77), the Allegheny County Courthouse, Pittsburgh (1884–88), and the Marshall Field Wholesale Store, Chicago (1885–87). Their progeny pervaded the American landscape, as in the Federal Courthouse at Oxford.

A related, smaller Victorian building that Faulkner knew well, just west of the Square, was the law office of his friend Phil Stone, built before the Civil War by the attorney William Sullivan. The Victorian tower at the front was added around the turn of the century (Fig. 72). Later Faulkner described a structure almost identical to it, though located in Cambridge, Massachusetts, in the Quentin section of *The Sound and the Fury*: *We went down the street and turned into a bit of lawn, in which, set back from the street, stood a one-storey building of brick trimmed with white. We went up . . . to the door and entered a bare room smelling of stale tobacco.*[6]

The most peculiar Mississippi Victorian pile to penetrate Faulkner's consciousness was not in Oxford but in Ripley—the home of his own great-grandfather, Colonel

FIGURE 71
Old Library (1889) and Confederate
Monument (1906), University of
Mississippi, Oxford.

FIGURE 72
Law Office of Phil Stone, Oxford, Mississippi (1850s, 1890s).

William Clark Falkner. After Falkner's antebellum house was burned by Union troops in 1863, he lived, according to his biographer, in "a simple, trim, one-storey building, modeled in plain good taste." In 1884, however, he completely transformed that building with the addition of two large new storeys (Figs. 73, 74). The resulting "Italian Villa," as it was called in Ripley, reflected the title, the content, and the sources of his recent, and final, book, *Rapid Ramblings in Europe* (1884), a revision of travel letters he had written the year before to his friend and kinsman, Thomas Spight, editor of the *Southern Sentinel,* who published them there.[7]

Falkner's newly enlarged house was inspired apparently by several villas and castles he had admired in Italy and France. Jammed on top of the original house, the new, slightly recessed, second floor sported four large gables, one on each side, containing French doors that opened to balconies decorated with ornate wrought-iron railings. Above this floor, in another recession, rose a large square room at the top, fenestrated with both rectangular and round porthole windows and crowned with a French Mansard roof topped by a "widow's walk." A contemporary notice in the Jackson *Clarion* asserted that Falkner "has built a residence that is quite palatial in style and proportions. Bel Haven excepted, there is no residence at the state capital that can compare with it." Ripley historian Andrew Brown, however, contrasted the exuberant facade with the plain, unexceptional interior: "The outward ostentation of the house, compared to its commonplace interior, makes one wonder if its building did not show that the Colonel's love of show was beginning to overrule his judgment." A later observer simply called the house an "architectural monster."[8]

Some of the house's furnishings echoed this judgment, particularly a stuffed alligator, caught in the Florida swamplands by the Colonel's daughter Effie and brought back to Memphis to be filled with sawdust by a taxidermist. Fixed to stand incongruously upright on its hind legs, the creature stood in the Falkners' front hall, with extended claws holding a large seashell intended to receive the calling cards of the Ripley gentry who called upon the Falkners (Fig. 75). Directly across the street, however, Falkner built a more felicitous and gracefully proportioned house as a wedding gift for his daughter, Willie Medora Falkner Carter (Fig. 102). Though William Faulkner knew his great-grandfather's house when he was a child in Ripley, and later when he visited there, he left no specific recollections of it and made no direct references to it in his work. He did leave a poignant record, however, of a childhood experience that occurred at his Aunt Willie's house across the street. (See Appendix, p. 141.)[9]

FIGURE 73

Falkner House, Ripley, Mississippi (1884).

FIGURE 74

Above: Courthouse Square, Ripley, Mississippi, Falkner House in center distance (ca. 1920).

FIGURE 75

Left: Stuffed Alligator from Falkner House, Ripley, Mississippi (ca. 1880s).

Faulkner did not admire postbellum Victorian Mississippi architecture, at least not in its residential forms. He used it in his work to symbolize the varied anxieties of the postwar New South, either as an example of parvenu social climbing or of resigned old guard resolution to accommodate the new order.

In *Sartoris,* a novel that is packed with architectural symbolism, Faulkner described a house built in Jefferson by an aspiring "hill-man" from the county, who had bought a beautifully planted lot in town *and cut some of the trees in order to build his house near the street after the country fashion. . . . The lot had been the site of a fine old colonial house which stood among magnolias and oaks and flowering shrubs. But the house had burned, and some of the trees had been felled to make room for an architectural garbling so imposingly terrific as to possess a kind of majesty. It was a monument to the frugality (and the mausoleum of the social aspirations of his women) of a hill-man who had moved in from a small settlement called French-man's Bend and who, as Miss Jenny Du Pre put it, had built the handsomest house in Frenchman's Bend on the most beautiful lot in Jefferson. The hill-man had stuck it out for two years, during which his womenfolk sat on the veranda all morning in lace-trimmed "boudoir caps" and spent the afternoons in colored silk, riding about town in a rubber-tired surrey; then the hill-man sold his house to a newcomer to the town and took his women back to the country and doubtless set them to work again.*[10]

Eventually, of course, these excessive Victorian concoctions became venerable monuments on the Mississippi landscape and occasionally, like their neoclassical neighbors, became myth-laden ruins. Faulkner's most famous evocation of such a condition occurred in his story "A Rose for Emily," where, as the Mississippi writer Elizabeth Spencer put it: a sweet little Southern lady, Miss Emily Grierson, poisoned her lover and "kept his corpse around as a playmate." Here, once again, as he did throughout his work, Faulkner used the style, setting, and condition of a building to evoke the condition of its inhabitants: *It was a big, squarish frame house that had once been white, decorated with cupolas and spires and scrolled balconies in the heavily lightsome style of the seventies, set on what had once been our most select street. But garages and cotton gins had encroached and obliterated even the august names of that neighborhood; only Miss Emily's house was left, lifting its stubborn and coquettish decay above the cotton wagons and gasoline pumps—an eyesore among eyesores.*[11]

Though Faulkner was uneasy with most Mississippi Victorian architecture, he had kind, and emotionally saturated, words for the Yoknapatawpha County jail, an important building in both Oxford's and Jefferson's history. Faulkner imagined the Jefferson jail to be older than the one in Oxford, which was actually built in 1871, possibly

FIGURE 76

Oxford Jail, Oxford, Mississippi (1871).

designed by Willis, Sloan, and Trigg, who designed the second courthouse, with similar decorative features, at approximately the same time (Fig. 76). In both Oxford and Jefferson, the jail retained an impressive presence on the landscape until it was needlessly demolished in the 1970s, just as it reached its centennial year. In *Intruder in the Dust,* Faulkner captured the essence of the actual, and the apocryphal, building in one of his most memorable paeans to the power and importance of architecture: *It was of brick, square, proportioned,* with columns *across the front and even a brick cornice under the eaves because it was old, built in a time when people took time to build even jails with grace and care and he remembered how his uncle had said once that not courthouses nor even churches but jails were the true records of a county's, a community's history, since not only the cryptic forgotten initials and words and even phrases cries of defiance and indictment scratched into the walls but the very bricks and stones themselves held, not in solution but in suspension, intact and biding and potent and indestructible, the agonies and shames and griefs with which hearts long since unmarked and unremembered dust had strained and perhaps burst.*[12]

Eight

"SPACIOUS, SUAVE, SONOROUS, AND MONASTIC"
The Modernist Architecture of Yoknapatawpha

William Faulkner, the literary modernist, was generally unsympathetic to the modern movement in architecture, a phenomenon not unique in the history of twentieth century modernist culture. Though certain avant-garde writers, painters, sculptors, composers, and architects eagerly embraced parallel developments in related fields, others were unable or unwilling to make the connections. To a certain extent, this antipathy was true for such writers as James Joyce and T. S. Eliot, and it was even more markedly the case with Faulkner. Like them, Faulkner seemed unable to identify his own literary experiments in cubistic simultaneity with related revolutions in painting, sculpture, and architecture.

Modernist architecture, like the other modernist arts, arose from a variety of sources and venues in the late nineteenth century, but few historians of the subject would question the assertion that a major source of activity was the burgeoning city of Chicago, which seized the opportunity for new techniques and forms after the Great Fire of 1871 necessitated an almost complete rebuilding of the central city. Led by such visionary pioneers as Daniel Burnham, John Root, and Louis Sullivan, the resulting "Chicago School" of skyscraper architecture forged the development of the epochal steel frame and of the modernist credo that the form of a building should express and articulate its function, its structural essence, and its meaning in time and place. In the early twentieth century, Sullivan's disciple Frank Lloyd Wright, and his so-called Prairie School, transferred the structural and aesthetic principles of skyscraper design

FIGURE 77

Beanland-Young House, Oxford, Mississippi (ca. 1905).

FIGURE 78

Beanland-Young House, interior.

to the private residence and the smaller public building and conveyed the "Chicago" principles of elegantly simple, functional modernism to the world.

Unlike the literary modernism of Joyce, Eliot, and Faulkner, which quoted richly from the whole history of civilization, architectural modernism moved from the late nineteenth century in a relatively more determined line toward the "pure," "new," and "original" forms of the International Style and its kindred mode, the Streamlined Moderne, of the 1920s and 1930s. Though most architects of these persuasions seemed to be striving for a transcendence of things past, many modernists were enamored of the elegant austerity of classical Japanese design and of the stark, white, skeletal ruins of antiquity. Yet the dominant references of the new twentieth-century architecture were the more consciously contemporary images of the Machine Age—as allied to, and expressive of, the conditions and "functions" of "modern life." Though most Mississippians, like Faulkner himself, professed a disdain for modernist architecture, the medium nevertheless made its way into the state. In 1889, two of Frank Lloyd Wright's earliest "Shingle Style" house designs were built facing the Gulf, side by side in Ocean Springs, Mississippi. One of these was a vacation house for Wright's mentor, Louis Sullivan. In the early twentieth century, the popularized versions of Wright's Prairie School and the kindred Craftsman-style bungalows of the designer Gustav Stickley could be found in Oxford and Ripley and most small Mississippi towns. Both types were usually filled with the familiar Craftsman or "Mission" furniture of Stickley and his followers.

In Oxford, the Beanland-Young house (ca.1905), built by a modest tailor, Edward Beanland, later mayor of Oxford, nestled among its neoclassical and Victorian neighbors on stately South Lamar. It represented, with its unencumbered horizontal lines, its low-slung hipped roof, and its darkly handsome interior paneling, a vaguely regional version of the Craftsman-influenced Prairie style. In certain variants, it was known as the "four-square" style (Figs. 77 and 78). In Ripley, on "Quality Ridge," near the older homes of the Thurmond, Murry, Falkner, Hines, and Spight families, the related Bostwick family, in the early 1920s, built a large, brick, one-storey, up-to-date version of the low-slung Craftsman bungalow, a mode that appeared in variant versions throughout most Mississippi, and American, towns.

In the 1930s especially, local Mississippi versions of the stark International Style and the more ebullient, curvilinear Streamlined Moderne became the style of choice for

FIGURE 79

Columbia High School, Columbia, Mississippi, Overstreet and Town, architects (1937).

federally funded projects of the New Deal's Works Progress Administration (WPA) and its related "alphabet-soup" recovery agencies. Of particular eminence among Mississippi architectural firms who worked in these idioms was the Jackson office of Overstreet and Town, who throughout the 1930s designed brilliant buildings that gained national recognition, including the superb Columbia High School, Columbia, Mississippi (Fig. 79); Bailey Junior High School, Jackson, Mississippi (Fig. 80); and such fetching, if modest, structures as a hospital for the small Delta town of Rosedale.

The style reached Oxford, not in a building by Overstreet and Town, but by their gifted colleague, James T. Canizaro (1904–1982), who in 1938 designed a small modernist gem in the WPA-sponsored Oxford City Hall (Figs. 81 and 82). Canizaro, a native of Vicksburg, studied architecture at Notre Dame in the late 1920s, after which he worked in the great Chicago office of Graham, Anderson, Probst, and White, the successor firm to the pioneering D.H. Burnham and Company. In the early 1930s,

Bailey Junior High School, Jackson, Mississippi, Overstreet and
Town, architects (1936).

Canizaro traveled to Europe where he made pilgrimages to, and photographic records
of, the modernist masterworks of Walter Gropius and other members of the German
Bauhaus school. In the mid-1930s he returned to his native state, where in Jackson,
the capital, he rented office space from the more established firm of Overstreet and
Town. He was especially close, both professionally and personally, to Hayes Town,
and the aesthetic affinities were obvious in his work. In a state where the capital was
the only place that seemed remotely urban, Canizaro knew that, in the beginning at
least, he would have to seek work in small-town Mississippi, and he thus began to
cultivate connections when and wherever he could.

In 1937, Canizaro obtained a commission in Oxford to design a sleekly modernist
concrete apartment house on University Avenue at South 11th Street, a mildly regional
version of the radical International Style. With the completion of this building, he told
his colleague Henry Mitchell, he won the friendship and support of Oxford mayor

Robert X. Williams, councilman Branham Hume, and such civic leaders as business-man Will Lewis. This no doubt facilitated his winning the commission to design the city hall, a structure that pushed even more courageously toward the brave new world of international modernism.[1]

Above two round modernist columns supporting the covered first floor entrance porch, the defining motif of the building was a long, thin band of contiguous ribbon windows, curving smartly at the corner in a quintessentially modernist gesture. To the right and on the axis of this key design element was an asymmetrically placed clock of chic modernist design. Below the clock was a metal tablet relating the history of Oxford in a stylish moderne typeface, a summary, in effect, of the history of Yokna-patawpha. This typeface was repeated in a magnified form in the letters over the front entrance announcing the name of the building. Connected to the hall on its northwest side was the Oxford Fire Department, whose up-to-date engines and firefighting equipment seemed appropriately at home within the streamlined architecture. Like

FIGURE 82
City Hall, Oxford.

his fellow Mississippi modernist William Faulkner, Canizaro was experimenting with brave new forms—nudging his state against its will, with Sisyphean commitment, into the modern world.

Except for the Moderne movie marquee of the Ritz Theater, just west of the Square, Canizaro's apartment house on University Avenue, the Holley Auto Garage on Van Buren Avenue (ca. 1930; Fig. 83), and the Art Deco facade of Ruth's Dress Shop on the Square, the first air-conditioned store in Oxford (1938; Fig. 84), the suave City Hall was the only visible architectural evidence that Lafayette County existed in the mid-twentieth century. Faulkner probably detested it, as did most of tradition-drenched Oxford. In the 1970s, the building, lacking supporters, was demolished and replaced by a blandly undistinguished structure for a new federal court and post office building, with a trade-off conversion of the old Federal Building into the Oxford City Hall. The needless demolition of Canizaro's gem suggested that twentieth-century Oxonians were less architecturally adventurous than their nineteenth-century prede-

FIGURE 83

Holley Garage, Oxford, Mississippi (ca. 1930, demolished).

FIGURE 84

Ruth's Dress Shop, Courthouse Square, east side, Oxford, Mississippi (1938, demolished).

cessors, none of whom apparently protested an architectural evolution resulting in the integrated diversity of pioneer log houses, Greek Revival mansions, Gothic Revival churches, Italianate villas and Richardsonian Romanesque federal buildings.

Though Faulkner never referred explicitly to Canizaro's building in his work, he probably would have agreed with the evaluation of it by the critic Ward Miner, who visited Mississippi in the early 1950s and, in his short, pioneering book, *The World of William Faulkner,* made flawed but insightful attempts to relate Oxford to Jefferson. The City Hall, Miner argued, was "an angular, garishly modern structure. . . . It is unfortunate that such a design was chosen, since it clashes with the rest of the community." In *Sanctuary,* Faulkner had used similar imagery to denote perversity and disequilibrium, as he observed the manner in which Popeye *walked, his tight suit and stiff hat all angles, like a modernistic lampstand.*[2]

The only types of modernist buildings to which Faulkner seemed sympathetic were urban skyscrapers and structures connected with airports. Long addicted to aviation, he celebrated the hangars of the New Valois airport in *Pylon* as *steel and glass caverns* with the main building emerging as unabashedly *modernistic, spacious, suave, sonorous, and monastic,* the latter a reference to its minimalist austerity. In its *bronze and chromium* lobby, the building's interior murals presented the *furious, still, and legendary tale of what man has come to call his conquering of the infinite and impervious air.* Though "New Valois" suggested New Orleans, a contemporary model closer to home was the new, modernist Memphis Airport, which Faulkner knew well (1938; Fig. 85).

In fact, the exceptions to Faulkner's antimodernist bias seemed to lie only in his fascination with airports and with very tall buildings. In *The Sound and the Fury,* he had his sensitive alter ego Quentin Compson remark, with apparent pleasure: *Father brought back a watch-charm from the Saint Louis Fair to Jason: a tiny opera glass into which you squinted with one eye and saw a skyscraper.*[4]

Indeed, Faulkner came closest to being seduced by modernism in the *purposeful* excitement and traffic of the city. In *Sanctuary* and particularly in the story "Dull Tale," he seemed to celebrate the modern urban environment: *Where Madison Avenue joins Main Street, where the trolleys swing crashing and groaning down the hill at the clanging of bells which warn and consummate the change of light from red to green, Memphis is almost a city.* At the intersection of Main and Madison, *where four tall buildings quarter their flanks and form an upended tunnel up which the diapason of traffic echoes as at the bottom of a well, there is the restless life and movement of cities; the hurrying and purposeful going to-and-fro* (Fig. 86).[5]

Main Building, Memphis Airport, Memphis, Tennessee, Walk
Jones Sr. and Walk Jones Jr., architects (1938), with earlier
hangars.

Faulkner was more ambivalent about another modernist intrusion onto the Yoknapatawpha landscape: the vast New Deal flood-control project (1938–42) that dammed
the Tallahatchie River and created Sardis Lake, an artificial reservoir that covered
hundreds of square miles in western Lafayette and eastern Panola counties. The dam
itself was a giant, mile-long mound of earth, one of the world's largest, with sculptur-
ally modernist steel and concrete elements framing the spillway and the water level
control towers (fig. 87). With handsome irony, these modernist totems hauntingly
echoed the predecessor structures of Indian mound and grain silo, now submerged in
the high water months, their tops reemerging as the lake subsided. In the late 1950s,
Faulkner's friend Ella Sommerville remarked wistfully and ironically that much of her
family's farm property was now at the bottom of Sardis Lake, as—alas—"Sutpen's
Hundred" would also have been. It was the fateful merger of two mythical worlds—
Yoknapatawpha and Atlantis.[6]

Faulkner himself loved to sail on Sardis Lake and to fish and hunt in its marshy
backwaters, where he must have been moved by the islandlike tops of the vestigial

FIGURE 86

Main Street, Memphis, Tennessee (late 1920s).

FIGURE 87

Sardis Dam and Sardis Lake, Panola and Lafayette counties
(1938–42).

Chickasaw mounds. In his fiction, strangely enough, he never exploited the fertile potential of this modernist inundation, though in his great prose poem "Mississippi," he evoked it with irony and pathos: *And now the young man, middle-aged now or anyway middle-aging, is back home, too, where they who altered the swamps and forests of his youth have now altered the face of the earth itself; what he remembered as dense river-bottom jungle and rich farmland is now an artificial lake twenty-five miles long: a flood-control project for the cotton fields below the huge earth dam . . . loving it even while hating some of it: the river jungle and the bordering hills, where still a child, he had ridden behind his father on the horse after the bobcat or fox or coon or whatever was ahead of the belling hounds and where he had hunted alone when he got big enough to be trusted with a gun—all this now the bottom of a muddy lake being raised gradually and steadily every year by another layer of beer cans and bottle caps and lost bass plugs.*[7]

With the exception of the airplane, Faulkner professed to hate machines—the automobile, radio, phonograph, and television—and he associated them—correctly—with what he considered the equally intrusive forces of architectural modernity. He seemed, indeed, to regret not only the appearance of modernism but even more the disappearance of the world it sometimes replaced. However admirably left-of-center Faulkner may have been on such crucial social issues as race relations, in most other ways he was dauntingly conservative. In the summer of 1927, for example, there was a concerted effort by the Oxford town fathers to pave the major streets. No longer would citizens have to walk through inches of mud on the square left after every rain (Fig. 88). Most Oxonians were delighted, but one—William Faulkner—opposed it because he saw it as the breaking of another link with the past.

In *Sanctuary*, written about the time of these improvements, he spoke through his character Horace Benbow in an unabashedly nostalgic homage to textures, shapes, and colors lost: *The street was narrow, quiet. It was paved now, though he could remember when, after a rain, it had been a canal of blackish substance, half earth, half water, with murmuring gutters in which he and Narcissa paddled and splashed with tucked-up garments and muddy bottoms, after the crudest of whittled boats, or made loblollies by treading and treading in one spot with the intense oblivion of alchemists. He could remember when, innocent of concrete, the street was bordered on either side by paths of red brick tediously and unevenly laid and worn in rich, random maroon mosaic into the black earth which the noon sun never reached; at that moment, pressed into the concrete near the entrance of the drive, were the prints of his and his sister's naked feet in the artificial stone.*[8]

Faulkner was understandably depressed in the 1940s by the demolition of some of the second floor porches around the Square, and he was even more disturbed by the needless destruction of the antebellum Cumberland Presbyterian Church on South Lamar Street. In protest, for years he refused to enter the modernist Kroger Grocery Store that replaced it. And the recurring rumors that the "inefficient" courthouse might be replaced he found unthinkable. He must have grimaced at the ungainly extensions to its east and west sides that were made to the building in the 1950s. In *Requiem for a Nun*, he expressed the fear that *every few years the county fathers, dreaming of bakshish, would institute a movement to tear it down and erect a new modern one, but someone would at the last moment defeat them; they will try it again of course and be defeated perhaps once again or even maybe twice again, but no more than that. . . . [I]ts doom is its longevity.*[9]

In *Requiem*, appropriately, he chanted a requiem for the old environment, mourning the losses with unabashed chauvinism: *gone now from the fronts of the stores are the old brick made of native clay in Sutpen's architect's old molds, replaced now by sheets of glass taller than*

FIGURE 89

Reflections of the Confederacy, Courthouse Square, Oxford,
Mississippi (1950s).

a man and longer than a wagon and team, pressed intact in Pittsburgh factories and framing interiors bathed now in one shadowless corpse-glare of fluorescent light; and now and at last, the last of silence too: the county's hollow inverted air one resonant boom and ululance of radio: and thus no more Yoknapatawpha's air nor even Mason and Dixon's air, but America's: the patter of comedians, the baritone screams of female vocalists, the babbling pressure to buy and buy and still buy arriving more instantaneous than light, two thousand miles from New York and Los Angeles. (Fig. 89).[10]

In fact, Faulkner's disinclination to appreciate the social and aesthetic significance of modernist architecture was no doubt one of the reasons he failed to identify with Los Angeles, the venue, next to Oxford, where he spent the largest part of his professional life. Living there periodically, he claimed, only to make money writing screenplays, he was unmoved by the fact that Southern California was one of the world's most important repositories of twentieth-century modernism. Because he failed to appreciate this, Faulkner chose to focus on the frequently ridiculous mimetic architecture of the area, the historicist cacophony of pseudo-French chateaux, English castles, and Egyptian tombs that echoed the movie sets of the Hollywood backlot. Hence, Los Angeles, or "Hollywood," as Faulkner referred to it, seemed shallow, rootless, and artificial. While numerous significant film-industry figures, such as directors Albert Lewin and Josef von Sternberg and producer Carl Laemmle, commissioned important modernist buildings from such avant-garde architects as Richard Neutra, Faulkner shared the popular image of Hollywood taste as confined to historicist kitsch. Faulkner was not alone in condemning such fakery. Like his fellow novelist Nathanael West, he disparaged the jerry-built, false-front follies that pervaded the area. In Faulkner's short story "Golden Land," for example, the buildings of Los Angeles County were *scattered about the arid earth like so many scraps of paper blown without order.* Indeed, had he been more disposed to appreciate modernist architecture, Faulkner's view of Los Angeles and the years he lived there might have been a more balanced one.[11]

Though Faulkner generally disapproved of modernism, he took an even grimmer view of antique reproductions, the sphere, in Yoknapatawpha, of the upstart, parvenu Snopeses. In *The Mansion,* he drolly satirized popular images of Southern architectural grandeur in the Snopes's "renovation" of the old de Spain house, which, with all its new "colyums," still *wouldn't be as big as Mount Vernon . . . but then Mount Vernon was a thousand miles away so there wasn't no chance of invidious or malicious eye to eye comparison.*

FIGURE 90

Avent Acres, Oxford, Mississippi (built late 1940s).

In *The Town, ever afternoon after the bank closed he would have to go and watch how the carpenters was getting along with his new house (it was going to have colyums across the front now, I mean the extry big ones so even a feller that never seen colyums before wouldn't have no doubt a-tall what they was, like in the photographs where the Confedrit sweetheart in a hoop skirt and a magnolia is saying good-bye to her Confedrit beau jest before he rides off to finish tending to General Grant).*[12]

Faulkner's snobbishness was less playful and hence less defendable in his disdain for the subdivision of the old estates and the building of plain, thoroughly respectable tract houses for families of modest income, as in Avent Acres, Oxford (Fig. 90). In *Requiem*, ominously, *there were new people in the town now, strangers, outlanders, living in new minute glass-walled houses set as neat and orderly and antiseptic as cribs in a nursery ward, in new subdivisions named Fairfield or Longwood or Halcyon Acres which had once been the lawn or back yard or kitchen garden of the old residencies (the old obsolete columned houses still standing among them like old horses surged suddenly out of slumber in the middle of a flock of sheep).*[13]

Faulkner was, at best, ambivalent to modernism, partially because the siting of new, modernist structures frequently seemed to call for the demolition of significant older ones. Though certain modernist phenomena clearly excited him, he mourned the related absence of what would come to be called a preservationist sensibility. In Yoknapatawpha and elsewhere, he was certain, there was an insufficient recognition of the power and presence of the past in the present. Perhaps, ironically, Faulkner could not understand that this also included the recent past and the monuments of the early modern movement, which, like all architecture, still constituted in the human experience the best example of the visible, tangible past.

Nine

"Each in Its Ordered Place"

The ultimate statement of Faulkner on architecture, on urban design, on the look and layout of Jefferson, had come early in his oeuvre, in a single passage from *Sartoris*, a passage that leads centrifugally to the Square, the center, the navel, of Yoknapatawpha:

They drove on and mounted the shady, gradual hill toward the square, and Horace looked about happily on familiar scenes. . . . Then a street of lesser residencies, mostly new. Same tight little houses with a minimum of lawn. . . . Then other streets opened away beneath arcades of green, shadier, with houses a little older and more imposing as they got away from the station's vicinity; and pedestrians, usually dawdling Negro boys at this hour or old men bound townward after their naps, to spend the afternoon in sober, futile absorptions. (Fig. 91)

The hill flattened away into the plateau on which the town proper had been built these hundred years and more ago, and the street became definitely urban presently with garages and small shops with merchants in shirt sleeves, and customers; the picture show with its lobby plastered with life episodic in colored lithographed mutations. Then the square, with its unbroken low skyline of old weathered brick and fading dead names stubborn yet beneath scaling paint, and drifting Negroes in casual and careless O.D. garments worn by both sexes, and country people in occasional khaki too; and the brisker urbanites weaving among their placid chewing unhaste and among the men in tilted chairs before the stores. (Plate 10, Figs. 92 and 93)

The courthouse was of brick too, with stone arches rising amid elms, and among the trees the monument of the Confederate soldier stood, his musket at order arms, shading his carven eyes with his stone hand. Beneath the porticoes of the courthouse and on benches about the green, the city

FIGURE 93

Vegetable Market, Courthouse Square, Oxford, Mississippi (late 1950s).

fathers sat and talked and drowsed, in uniform here and there. . . . When the weather was bad they moved inside to the circuit clerk's office (Fig. 94)[1]

For most of the twentieth century, traffic on the Oxford Square has drifted lazily to the right, but in the early twentieth century, one could go either counterclockwise to the right or clockwise to the left. Yet Benjy Compson, the retarded Compson son in *The Sound and the Fury*, had an aversion to the clockwise direction, a strong need for the anticlockwise course, perhaps a symbol of Faulkner's for Benjy's problems with time and history; perhaps too a suggestion that soon the whole town, and much of the universe, would be following the same course. Indeed the utterly idyllic portrayal of the Square in *Sartoris* contrasted markedly with the last two pages of *The Sound and the Fury*, where the dark decline of the Compson family erupted symbolically at the same Courthouse Square beneath the same Confederate monument. Still, it is significant that that brilliantly told tale of chaos and decline ends on the final page with a suggestion of order, a suggestion that Faulkner rendered in architectural terms: *They approached the square, where the Confederate soldier gazed with empty eyes beneath his marble hand into wind and weather. Luster took another notch in himself and gave the impervious*

FIGURE 94

Second Lafayette County Courthouse, Willis, Sloan, and Trigg,

architects (ca. 1870; postcard, early twentieth century).

Queenie a cut with the switch, casting his glance about the square. . . . Ben sat, holding the flower in his fist, his gaze empty and untroubled. Luster hit Queenie again and swung her to the left at the monument.

For an instant Ben sat in an utter hiatus. Then he bellowed. Bellow on bellow, his voice mounted, with scarce interval for breath. There was more than astonishment in it, it was horror; shock; agony eyeless, tongueless; just sound, and Luster's eyes back-rolling for a white instant. "Gret God," he said, "Hush! Hush! Gret God!" He whirled again and struck Queenie with the switch. It broke and he cast it away and with Ben's voice mounting toward its unbelievable crescendo Luster caught up the end of the reins and leaned forward as Jason came jumping across the square and onto the step.

With a backhanded blow he hurled Luster aside and caught the reins and sawed Queenie about . . . while Ben's hoarse agony roared about them, and swung her about to the right of the monument. Then he struck Luster over the head with his fist. "Don't you know any better than to take him to the left?" he said. He reached back and struck Ben, breaking the flower stalk again. "Shut up!" he said "Shut up!" He jerked Queenie back and jumped down. . . . "Yes, suh!" Luster said. He took the reins and hit Queenie with the end of them. . . . Ben's voice roared

FIGURE 95

Confederate Monument, Courthouse Square, Oxford, Mississippi
(1907).

and roared. Queenie moved again, her feet began to clop-clop steadily again, and at once Ben hushed. Luster looked quickly back over his shoulder, then he drove on. The broken flower drooped over Ben's fist and his eyes were empty and blue and serene again as cornice and facade flowed smoothly once more from left to right; post and tree, window and doorway, and signboard, each in its ordered place (Fig. 95).[2]

Thus, in work after work, Faulkner answered resoundingly the question he had posed long before in *Mosquitoes* in asserting and demonstrating that architecture was not only *a part of life* but an art that shaped and reflected its contours. However great the pain and joy of *the comedy and tragedy of being alive,* architecture was an art that was fundamental to life. Among all the vagaries of art and of life, it came closest to representing a sense of continuity between the past and the present. Indeed, it was—in Jefferson, the town—surely among the things that made up the quest for what Jefferson the man, Jefferson the architect had called "the pursuit of happiness."

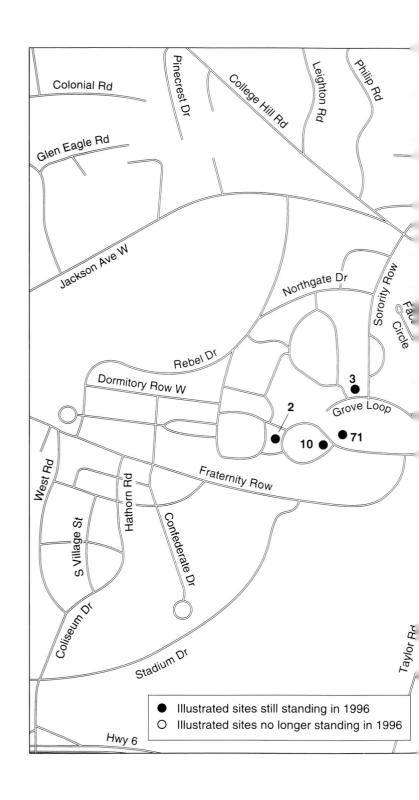

Colonial Rd

Pinecrest Dr

College Hill Rd

Leighton Rd

Philip Rd

Glen Eagle Rd

Jackson Ave W

Northgate Dr

Sorority Row

Fau- Circle

Rebel Dr

Dormitory Row W

2

3

Grove Loop

10

71

West Rd

S Village St

Hathorn Rd

Confederate Dr

Fraternity Row

Coliseum Dr

Stadium Dr

Taylor Rd

● Illustrated sites still standing in 1996
○ Illustrated sites no longer standing in 1996

Hwy 6

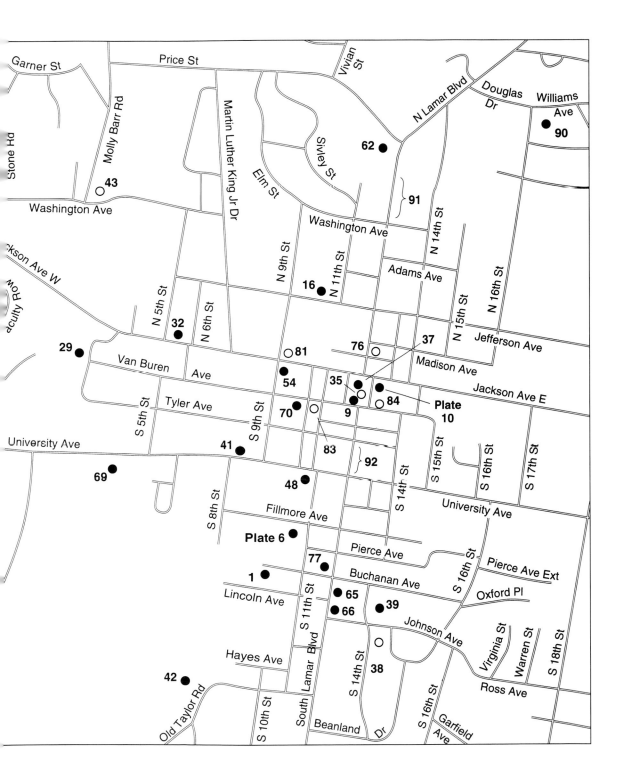

FIGURE 96

Map of Oxford, Mississippi.

Map 1.
Mississippi

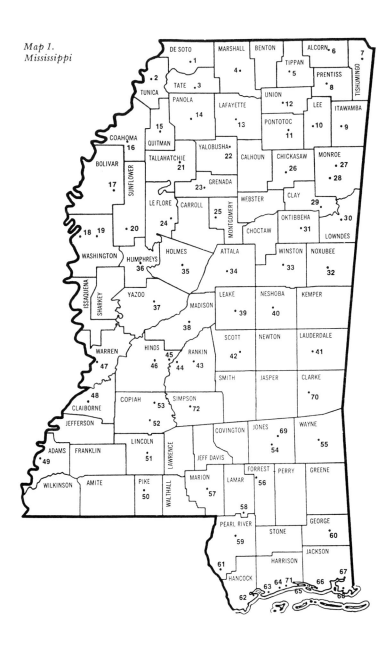

FIGURE 97

County Map of Mississippi (Ripley, 5; Oxford, 13; New Albany,
12; Columbus, 30; Holly Springs, 4; Jackson, 45; Columbia,
57; Port Gibson, 48).

Appendix

To: Taylor Spight Hines
From: Thomas Spight Hines
Re: William Faulkner and the relationship of the Spight, Hines, and Fa(u)lkner families
18 April 1994

Dear Taylor:

As you have begun to read and admire the work of William Faulkner, you have asked me on several occasions to share with you my personal memories of Faulkner when I was growing up in Oxford, Mississippi, and of the long relationship that our family has had with his. So I am turning to this before my memory gets any dimmer. Consider this a belated eighteenth birthday present.

My earliest sense of Faulkner came from my father's recollections of his and his family's world as it intersected with that of the Falkners in Ripley and Tippah County, Mississippi, in the nineteenth and early twentieth centuries. (For reasons that have never been totally clear, Faulkner added the "u" to the family name in the 1920s.) Throughout my early life, I went back to Ripley with my parents at least two or three times a year to visit relatives, particularly at family funerals, which in rural Mississippi were usually warm and frequently festive occasions. These reunions included primarily branches of the Hines and Spight families, my father's mother, Mattie Spight Hines, having been the daughter of Thomas Spight, a cousin of Holland Pearce Falkner, William's great-grandmother.

These family gatherings included not only people still dwelling in Ripley but far-flung relatives returning there to bury the dead, which means that the now rather dilapidated Ripley cemetery has a vivid place in my consciousness. On the hundreds of occasions I have visited it through the years, from the earliest to the most recent, I have never failed to walk from the Hines and Spight sections southeast to the tall statue over the grave of Colonel William Clark Falkner, William Faulkner's great-grandfather. I recall once when, as young children, we were obviously making too much noise, our Aunt Virginia suggested firmly that we "go over and count the books on Colonel Falkner's statue." The books were granite simulacra, stacked at his side, of the actual books he had written in life.

The best evocation of this scene is from Faulkner's novel *Sartoris,* in which the character of Colonel Sartoris is largely based on that of Colonel Falkner: *He stood on a stone pedestal, in his frock coat . . . one leg slightly advanced and one hand resting lightly on the stone pylon beside him. His head was lifted a little in that gesture of haughty pride which repeated itself generation after generation with a fateful fidelity, his back to the world and his carven eyes gazing out across the valley where his railroad ran and the blue, changeless hills beyond, and beyond that the ramparts of infinity itself.*

In addition to my father, the people who most enriched my sense of Ripley and the Spight-Hines-Falkner connection were two women, who in their different ways were both interesting and intelligent people: my great-aunt Nancy Spight, wife of Lindsey Donelson Spight (son of Thomas, brother of my grandmother, Mattie) and, as corrective counterpoint, Aunt Virginia Hines McKinney, my father's sister, who disapproved not only of William Clark Falkner and William Cuthbert Faulkner but also of Aunt Nancy herself, who was something of a family rival. Aunt Virginia was, for her time and place, a remarkably liberal Democrat (an avid Rooseveltian New Dealer and an admirer of Eleanor as well), but morally a pious Baptist who was repelled by *Sanctuary.* Aunt Nancy was less pious, but much more politically conservative; she greatly admired Senator Eastland, and she was an eager, and competent, DAR / UDC genealogist. The enclosed "family tree" is actually from Aunt Nancy's DAR chart, but her findings confirm and emend those of careful and reputable historians. For example, she established the fact that the first American Spight was one Ira Spight, who sailed from London to Virginia in July 1635.

The major Spight-Falkner connections in Mississippi in the nineteenth century resulted from the kinship of my great-grandfather, Thomas Spight, his uncle, Simon Reynolds Spight, and their cousin, Holland Pearce Falkner, the first wife of Colonel Falkner. The common ancestors of Thomas, Simon, and Holland were Mary Reynolds Spight (1760–1822), a relative of the English painter Sir Joshua Reynolds, and Simon Spight (1741–1816), a quartermaster in the Revolutionary Army. Simon was a cousin of Richard Dobbs Spaight (1758–1802), a signer of the United States Constitution and the third governor of North Carolina. (In those days, different branches of various families spelled their surnames differently.) Simon and Mary Spight lived and died in Jones County, North Carolina, and never saw Mississippi. Their children included Holland Spight Harrison, Faulkner's ancestor, and the first Mississippi Thomas Spight (1779–1857), my great-great-great-grandfather. Spight migrated from North Carolina in 1830 to Gibson County, Tennessee, and along with another of Faulkner's great-great-grandfathers, Abel Vance Murry, was one of the original white settlers of Tippah County after the Chickasaws ceded these lands in the Treaty of Pontotoc (1832). Spight's obituary states that in 1836, the year of its founding, he "moved to this county, then in the occupation of the Indians." One of the witnesses to his will was Richard J. Thurmond, Colonel Falkner's future business partner and assassin.

The Spight and Faulkner lines in question run like this:

1. Simon Spight md. Mary Reynolds.
children: Thomas, Holland, Ira, Sharpe,
Everett, and Mary

2. Holland Spight md. Simmon Harrison.
child: Elizabeth

2. Thomas Spight md. Rebecca Mumford.
children: James Mumford, Joseph Coleman,
and Simon Reynolds.

3. Elizabeth Harrison md. Joseph Pearce. children: Holland, Joseph, Lazarus, and Mary.

3. James Mumford Spight md. Mary Elizabeth Rucker. children: Thomas, Lindsey, Simon, and Fannie.

4. Holland Pearce md. William Falkner. child: John W. T.

4. Thomas Spight md. Mary Virginia Barnett. children: Lindsey, Henry, Virginia, Allie, Mamie, and Mattie.

5. J. W. T. Falkner md. Sallie Murry. children: John, Murry, and Holland.

5. Mattie Spight md. William Hines. children: William, Virginia, Chesley, Lillian, and Thomas.

6. Murry Falkner md. Maud Butler. children: William, Murry, John, and Dean.

6. Thomas Spight Hines md. Polly Moore. children: Thomas and Sally.

7. William Faulkner md. Estelle Oldham. children: Jill and Alabama.

7. Thomas Spight Hines, Jr. md. Dorothy Taylor. children: Taylor and Tracy.

(Between the first Simon Spight and the present, there has obviously been one more generation in our family than in the Falkner family, since my father's generation (6) and William Faulkner's generation (7) are obviously of the same age and time.)

In his novel *Sartoris,* Faulkner has John Sartoris proclaim: *In the nineteenth century genealogy is poppycock. Particularly in America, where only what a man takes and keeps has any significance, and where all of us have a common ancestry and the only house from which we can claim descent with any assurance is the Old Bailey. Yet the man who professes to care nothing about his forefathers is only a little less vain than he who bases all his actions on blood precedent* (p. 87).

Be that as it may, after the first Simon Spight, the common ancestor, the most important person in the Spight-Falkner connection—the person most responsible for bringing Holland Pearce to Ripley, where she met her future husband, W. C. Falkner, and bore his first son, J. W. T. Falkner—was Holland's cousin, Simon Reynolds Spight, son of the first Mississippi Thomas Spight and grandson of the North Carolina Simon Spight. According to Nancy Spight (in a letter to me, undated, ca. 1955), "Simon R. Spight, on the death of the father, became the guardian of the Pearce children." About the time that Holland Pearce married William Falkner, her brother, Joseph Pearce, married Frances (Fanny) Spight, the daughter of Simon. During these years, Aunt Nancy states, Thomas Spight and his sons James Mumford and Simon Reynolds "owned about 100 slaves." (I recall here, Taylor, that as you began to study American history in the Los Angeles schools, you were rightly shocked and dismayed to learn that you were, alas, a descendant of slaveholders!) Of Simon Reynolds Spight, Aunt Nancy also noted that: "Before the Civil War, there was a flood in Missouri. Levees broke and, without remuneration, he took his slaves and went to Mo. and helped to repair the damage. Many years later, the state of Mo. gave him some land . . . as their appreciation."

The historian Joel Williamson, in his fascinating book *William Faulkner and Southern History,* observed that "from local records, one can easily pick out the dozen or so clans that formed the elite, the 'aristocracy' of Tippah County and the town of Ripley. . . . Some clans, such as the Spights, maintained both plantations in the country and impressive households in town, and their sons might become lawyers and doctors" (p. 37). Unfortunately, Williamson did not know the actual family relationship of Holland Pearce and Simon R. Spight (as cousins and descendants of Simon Spight), but he wrote an otherwise cogent analysis of the implications of their relationship:

FIGURE 98

Simon Spight House, Ripley, Mississippi (1850s and later, demolished; photograph, late nineteenth century).

"Holland Pearce did not come at all empty handed to her marriage. Along with several siblings, she was an orphan who was in the process of collecting a substantial inheritance when she met William. Also, she was in some way connected to Simon R. Spight and his family. Both the Pearces and the Spights were originally from Jones County, North Carolina, a region of wealthy planters and slaveholders in the eastern part of the state. Simon Spight was primarily a merchant and hotel owner in Ripley; but he also owned land and slaves and would become one of the several richest men in the county during the 1850s. Very early in 1847, he became the guardian for Holland and her four brothers and sisters. Holland's father had died without a will in Weakley County, in northwestern Tennessee, leaving a large estate that included twenty-eight slaves" (pp. 18–19).

Williamson then goes on to explain how "Simon Spight undertook the complicated business of settling affairs in Tennessee and moving the Pearce children to Ripley. He bought and sold slaves during the division of property in Tennessee, in one case making a purchase to keep Jim and Rachel and their one-year-old daughter together as a family. Also, he hired people and transportation to move the Pearces, their effects, and their slaves to Ripley, a twenty-seven-day journey by wagon and carriage. In January, 1847, he leased out for the year the employable slaves for $1,088, keeping the unemployables in his own household. During that year, at a cost that exceeded their income, he maintained the Pearce children and saw to their education."

FIGURE 99

Chesley Hines House, Ripley, Mississippi (1850s and later, demolished) railroad tracks in foreground.

On July 9, 1847, Holland Pearce and William Falkner were married in Knoxville, Tennessee—
the area in which she had lived before moving to Ripley and in which, presumably, she still had
relatives. On September 2, 1848, a son, John Wesley Thompson Falkner, was born. Holland died of
consumption in the spring of 1849. In 1851, Falkner married Elizabeth Vance, and they subsequently
had six children: William Henry, Thomas Vance, Lizzie Manassah, Effie Deane, Willie Medora, and
Alabama Leroy, the latter two of whom were later connected to our family and to this story.

The major postwar Hines-Falkner connection involved the splendidly named Ship Island, Ripley
and Kentucky railroad, of which Falkner and Richard Thurmond each owned one-third of the stock.
Chesley Hines, my great-grandfather, and his brother-in-law, C. L. Harris, my great-great-uncle,
owned the other third, Hines owning slightly more than one-sixth. This was significant since Hines
usually tended to side and to vote with Falkner while Harris, a kinsman of Thurmond's, tended to
side with Thurmond—a situation that usually gave Falkner a slight edge. Chesley Hines (1834–1879)
was an enigmatic figure, in some ways not unlike William Falkner, in that (unlike the more established
and well-documented Spights), he seemed to "appear" in Ripley as something of a loner. He was
born in 1834 in Hardeman County, Tennessee, into a family who had come originally from the Caro-
linas. At the age of eleven, for reasons that are not clear, he left home, possibly as an orphan, and like
Falkner lived for a while with relatives in Missouri, before migrating south to Tippah County in 1852
at the age of eighteen. He did not, amazingly, attend school until he was twenty years old, but was
described as "an expert mathematician . . . a natural born mechanic," and a "practical accoun-

tant." In 1858, he married Elizabeth Harris, daughter of the prominent Onie Allen and John C. Harris, originally from neighboring Marshall County. Hines served in the Confederate army and was wounded at Perryville, Kentucky.

Chesley Hines's reputation as mechanic, accountant, and mathematician and, by the 1870s, his increasingly comfortable income made it logical for him to join Falkner's and Thurmond's railroad enterprise, which seems to have gotten under way in 1872. Historian Stewart H. Holbrook, in *The Story of American Railroads,* observed that Falkner apparently "got to thinking that Ripley, a mere backwoods hamlet to which freight had to be hauled by team, ought to have better contact with the world. Falkner did not have much capital, but he did possess eloquence, which in the South of that day was rated higher than capital, and he had an idea—a railroad from Ripley to tap the Memphis and Charleston at Middleton, Tennessee, twenty miles north. . . . He must have had a winning personality . . . for he got his fellow Mississippians, nearly all of them made poor by the war, to supply cash and other aid in plenty. Some cleared the right-of-way. Others furnished lumber and ties and timbers. Many turned out to lay the rails. Much of this was donated labor. Among those paying cash for stock were the Harris, the Hines, and other well-to-do families, but the heaviest stockholder of all came to be R. J. Thurmond" (pp. 144–45).

Chesley Hines seems to have been the partner most involved in the technical aspects of actually running the railroad. In 1879, he lost his life in an accident while piloting the train when a stray animal suddenly appeared on the track as it crossed a trestle between Ripley and the hamlet of Falkner, causing the engine to overturn. In the crash that followed, Chesley Hines was scalded to death. His widow, Elizabeth Harris Hines, mother of nine children, retained the stock as a silent partner, supplementing her income by transforming portions of the huge Hines house, just west of the train tracks and across from the depot, into the Ripley Hotel. Richard Thurmond was a bondsman for the estate. Later, Chesley's son William, my grandfather, worked as an engineer on the railroad and had the eerie experience of spotting an animal sauntering on to the tracks very near the spot where his father had been killed. Fortunately, he was able to stop the train in time to avoid his father's fate, but my father remembers him saying that, in his fright, his hair "stood up" beneath his cap.

This is not the place to go into the evolution of the Falkner-Thurmond feud, since it is ably analyzed, from different perspectives, by such scholars as Andrew Brown, Joseph Blotner, and Joel Williamson, except to say that my father remembers hearing the oft-noted contention, both in his family and out in Ripley, that *one* of the sources of friction involved questions about Elizabeth Hines's stock and her share of the dividends. My father's sense was that Falkner had sided with the widow Hines and had *possibly* insinuated that Thurmond, as one of the bondsmen for Chesley Hines's estate, had not treated her fairly. This is *somewhat* confirmed by Andrew Brown in his judicious *History of Tippah County, Mississippi* (p. 292). In documenting one of the public confrontations between Falkner and Thurmond prior to their final encounter, Brown quoted an eyewitness to the effect that "while Thurmond was talking to a group in the courthouse yard, Falkner walked up to him, thrust his hands into the armholes of his vest, and said, 'Well, here I am Dick. What do you want of me?' Thereupon Thurmond lashed out with his fist, knocking Falkner down. The infuriated Colonel rose to his feet and launched into a long tirade in which he accused Thurmond, among other things, of being a robber of widows and orphans. . . ." Whatever the prelude, the causes or motivations, the fact is that on November 5, 1889, Falkner was shot by Thurmond on the Ripley square, while talking with his friend Thomas Rucker, a cousin of Thomas Spight. He died the next day.

Indeed, in the latter part of William Falkner's life, Thomas Spight played as significant a role as his uncle, Simon Spight, had done in the earlier period when Falkner married Simon's cousin and legal

FIGURE 100

Tippah County Confederate Veterans Reunion, Company B, 34th
Infantry Regiment, Walthall's Brigade, C.S.A., Ripley, Mississippi
(1904). Thomas Spight, Company Commander, front row, 5th
from left, under flag; Ripley School in background.

ward, Holland Pearce. Like his grandfather and namesake, the first Mississippi Thomas Spight, and like Simon Spight as well, the second Thomas Spight (1841–1924) was, if not a prototype, at least a person who predicted and suggested certain clearly discernible aspects of later "Faulknerian" literary characters.

Thomas was born into what Blotner calls a "prominent" family and Williamson an "elite" family, the son of Mary Elizabeth Donelson Rucker and James Mumford Spight. He grew up in Ripley and on the Spight plantation east of town. He was a beginning student at La Grange Synodical College, La Grange, Tennessee, when the war began in 1861. Leaving college with his valet-factotum and lifelong companion Tucker Spight, a black slave of roughly his own age, "given" to him early in his life, Thomas Spight entered the Confederate army as a third lieutenant. Before he was twenty-one, he had advanced to the rank of captain, Company B, 34th Mississippi Infantry, Walthall's Brigade, a military experience that reached a fateful apex in the Battle of Atlanta, 1864, in which he was wounded. "Tuck" Spight apparently was crucial in saving his life by pulling him from the thick of battle into a nearby wood and getting medical aid for him. With Tuck at his side, he surrendered with his command at Greensboro, North Carolina, April 1865. For the rest of his life, Captain Spight, as he was thereafter known, walked with a limp and carried a cane. Tuck Spight accompanied him to the annual Confederate veterans reunions. Both men claimed, more than half seriously, that Tuck should be officially considered a "Confederate veteran."

After the war, Spight, "land poor" like most of his family, returned to Mississippi, first to farm and then to study law and begin his practice. In 1865, he married his first cousin, Mary Virginia Barnett. His and his wife's mothers were sisters, the daughters of Nancy Ann Kavanaugh and Henry Tate Rucker. Spight was one of the first former Confederates to get elected to the Mississippi House of Representatives (1874–80), where he was instrumental in the impeachment of the "carpetbag" governor Adelbert Ames. (Later in Washington, as a member of Congress, Spight's desk was next to that of Adelbert Ames's son.)

Following his legislative years, Spight resolved to continue his political career on a larger scale and, to this end, in 1879 he founded and became editor of the Ripley *Southern Sentinel.* He continued as editor until 1884 when he was elected district attorney, a post he would hold until 1892. The paper, which he continued to own and over which he maintained a paternalistic interest, would become one of the best weeklies in north Mississippi and would be especially valuable as the major documentary source for recording the life and development of Tippah County. Spight also used it to publish, serially, the last book of William Falkner. In 1883, a year after the publication of his novel *The Little Brick Church* and two years after the appearance of his most famous work, *The White Rose of Memphis,* Falkner decided to travel to Europe with his daughter Effie, and beginning with his arrival in New York, he began keeping a notebook of his experiences. He sent these notes back in the form of letters to his friend, Thomas Spight, and Spight published them in the paper in weekly installments—much as the rival Ripley paper, *The Advertiser,* had serially published *The White Rose of Memphis.* Upon his return, Falkner revised and expanded the sketches into a book he called *Rapid Ramblings in Europe,* which Lippincott published in 1884. In its drolly humorous picture of Americans in Europe, it resembles Mark Twain's *Innocents Abroad.* I have the copy of the book that Falkner presented to Spight.

By this time, the Spight and Falkner homes were diagonally across from each other. Thomas Spight's house, called "The Magnolias" after the large trees in front, faced Union Street between Cooper and Pine and was a Victorian remodeling of an older house that had been in the Spight family for some time. Falkner's more wildly eclectic "Italian villa" indeed reflected, with its overscaled Mansardic

FIGURE 101

Falkner House, Ripley, Mississippi
(1884, demolished; photograph
ca. 1900), view from front yard of
Captain Thomas Spight, his daughter, Lillian Spight, in foreground.

tower, his own "rapid ramblings in Europe." Occupying the whole block between Union, Cooper, Mulberry, and Main streets, it too was a remodeling of a smaller, older house. Between these two houses on the block facing Cooper, between Union and Main Streets, was the house Falkner built for his daughter Willie Medora and her husband, the physician N. G. Carter. While "The Magnolias" would continue to be occupied into the mid-twentieth century by Spight's unmarried daughters, Allie and Mamie, the Falkner and Carter houses would be sold to two of Thomas Spight's other children, Falkner's cousins-by-marriage: his own to Lindsey Donelson Spight, my father's uncle, and the Carter house to William and Mattie Spight Hines, my grandparents. More on the Carter-Hines house later.

Despite the kinship and friendship, however, there were sometimes tense moments between Spight and Falkner. In one of her letters to me in the mid-1950s, Aunt Nancy recalled, of Captain Spight, that: "One time he and Col. Falkner were arguing a case, and Col. Falkner called him a liar, it was said, there was a table between them and Capt. Spight jumped over but friends caught them before there was a fight. He went home to dinner and before he went back there was a note brought to him from Col. Falkner apologizing, which it seems was a compliment to both men. Col. Falkner was a hot head, I have always understood, and he must have had respect for Capt. Spight to apologize." Aunt Virginia also passed on a story about this incident to the effect that Spight's wife, my great-grand-mother, Mary Virginia, was so outraged by Falkner's accusation that in the hours between the confrontation and the apology she burned the first editions that Falkner had given them of *The White Rose of Memphis* and *The Little Brick Church.*

In the late 1880s, however, the Spight-Falkner relationship took on a new dimension as the Falkner-Thurmond relationship deteriorated. "Thurmond wanted only to be left alone," Andrew Brown contends, "though he was determined to defend himself if he thought his life was in danger. Falkner's attitude seems to have been one of fatalism. Late in 1889, he told Captain Spight, in the manner of one merely stating a fact, that Dick Thurmond was going to kill him, and asked some questions about preparing his will. Spight suggested that Falkner carry a gun for self-defense, but the Colonel refused to do so, saying that he had killed two men already, and had rather die himself than slay another" (pp. 292–93). Spight advised Falkner and probably made notes or a draft of the will that was written and witnessed in Memphis on October 25, 1889.

Though accounts of motivations and circumstances vary widely, Thurmond shot Falkner on the Ripley square on the following November 5th. Since his wife and younger children were not at the "villa" but in Memphis, and likely because his son-in-law was the town physician, Falkner was taken to the home of his daughter, Willie Medora Carter, across the street. There he died the following day. The funeral was at his wife's Presbyterian church, though Willie Carter latter commissioned a stained glass window for her own Baptist church, which the Baptists declined to install, ostensibly because Falkner was not a church member. Aunt Virginia claimed that Thurmond partisans threatened to destroy it if it were placed in the church. According to Brown, Mrs. Carter "finally placed it in the sitting room of her home, later known as the William Hines place, cutting through the back wall to make a place for it. It remained there for many years, long after the Carters had left Ripley" (p. 302). I can remember long ago seeing the window after the house was sold and no longer belonged to my family.

After the shooting, Thurmond was promptly jailed and indicted, but due to defense counsel's delaying tactics and to the general consensus that a cooling-off period was needed, Thurmond's trial for manslaughter did not begin until February 18, 1891. According to various witnesses, Thomas Spight, the district attorney, prosecuted the case vigorously. My grandfather, William Hines, was summoned to be a juror and then was dismissed because of a conflict of interests: he had just become engaged to be married to Spight's daughter Mattie. Thurmond hired the best criminal lawyers in the state to defend him, though the Falkner partisans also claimed that he used his vast wealth to "buy off" potential jurors as well. In any case, after a tense and complex trial, Thurmond was acquitted.

In 1892, Thomas Spight returned to the private practice of law while making plans for higher political office. In 1898, he was elected to Congress and remained there through the administrations of McKinley, Roosevelt, and Taft, being defeated for reelection in 1911 by supporters of the Populist James K. Vardaman. Though Spight's views on the race question seem conservative in retrospect, he was considered in his day to be left of center in such matters, having refused, for example, to join the Ku Klux Klan.

If not a great national leader, Spight was considered a distinguished Southern congressman. Yet nothing on the national agenda apparently seemed more important to him or took a higher priority than promoting Confederate veterans' affairs and unveiling and dedicating Confederate monuments. He dedicated the monuments in Ripley and Oxford, for which I still have manuscript copies of his rather impassioned speeches. While Spight was a member of Congress, he and his family had an apartment at the Willard Hotel. After leaving Washington, he returned to practice law in semiretirement in Ripley. One afternoon, after his lunch and nap, he returned to his office on the square and was baffled to find the street department taking down *his* Confederate monument. He did not understand that the roadway around the square was simply being improved and that the monument was going to be returned to its rightful place, but in his astonishment, he had a stroke and died. It was the end of a strikingly symmetrical life—for the Confederacy.

The house of Willie Medora Carter, in which Colonel Falkner died, would provide a small but poignant memory for her great-nephew, William Fa(u)lkner, born in 1897 in New Albany, Mississippi, where his father was working for the family-owned railroad. In 1898, the family moved back to Ripley, where they lived on Jackson Street until 1902, when they moved permanently to Oxford. The incident involved a childhood visit of William to his Aunt Willie's house two blocks away and was recalled in a letter he wrote from Paris, September 10, 1925, to his Aunt Bama McLean, Willie's sister, a letter that noted an anticipated visit with his cousin, Willie's daughter, Vance, called Vannye. *I will be*

FIGURE 102

Carter-Hines House, Ripley, Mississippi (1884, demolished).

awfully glad to see Vannye again, he wrote *The last time I remember seeing her was when I was 3, I suppose. I had gone to spend the night with Aunt Willie . . . and I was suddenly taken with one of those spells of loneliness and nameless sorrow that children suffer, for what or because of what they do not know. And Vannye and Natalie brought me home, with a kerosene lamp. I remember how Vannye's hair looked in the light—like honey* (Blotner, *Selected Letters,* p. 20).

My parents also passed on to me a story that Grandmother Hines had told them, which was confirmed and emended for me in the late 1950s by Faulkner's mother, "Miss Maud." Sometime during the years when Murry and Maud Falkner and their children lived in Ripley, my father's older brother, William Hines, and William Fa(u)lkner, a distant cousin and playmate roughly the same age, went off one afternoon to play together. At sunset, the two small boys had not returned and the families became rather worried. After cursory searches had revealed no boys, a formal searching party was organized and the two young Williams were found inside an old culvert, sound asleep, apparently exhausted from the day's play. Miss Maud said that she would never forget the anxiety she and my grandmother felt in the belief that something terrible had happened to their two oldest sons. I don't know how much the years added to the "awesomeness" of this incident but, on the other hand, the world might owe a lot to that searching party. Aunt Virginia, who was frequently a playmate of the two Williams, also recalled that her brother, William Hines, had a toy goat that made a noise that William Fa[u]lkner was afraid of. Whenever William H. would frighten William F. with the goat, the latter would go to my grandmother and say, "Miss Mattie, make William put up the Billy Goat."

When the Carters left Ripley in 1901 or 1902, they sold their house to my grandparents, William and Mattie Spight Hines. My father always seemed very proud of the fact that, in 1906, he was born in the same room in which Colonel Falkner had died. My grandmother lived there until her death in 1936, after which the house was rented for several years and then sold. In the 1960s, the current owners resold the land for commercial development, and this large, two-storey house was moved out into the country, east of Ripley, where, I am told, it became a crossroads store and "honky-tonk" before it burned several years later—a sadly ironic and, I am tempted to say, "Faulknerian" sequence of events.

My father grew up in Ripley, graduated from Ripley High School in 1923, received his B.A. degree in history from Mississippi College in 1927 and his M.A. degree in Latin from the University of Mississippi in 1935. After college, he taught Latin and History *and* coached football at Oxford High School, during which time he was a colleague of Dorothy Oldham, Estelle Faulkner's sister, who would become a lifelong friend. In the early 1930s, he moved to teach at Webb, in the Mississippi Delta, where he met and married my mother, Polly Moore, in 1932. They then returned to Oxford, where he continued to teach and coach at the renamed University High School, teaching there both Malcolm Franklin and Victoria ("Cho-cho") Franklin, children of Estelle Faulkner from her first marriage to Cornell Franklin. The Faulkners hosted several school parties and graduation functions for their children at their home, Rowan Oak, which my parents attended. My father recalled talking with Faulkner there and on other such occasions about Ripley and their various family connections.

My mother in those years also belonged to the same bridge club as Estelle Faulkner and recalled with a kind of bemused, mock horror that one afternoon when the club was meeting at Rowan Oak, with the ladies "dressed-up" in proper 1930s Oxford bridge-playing attire, William rather "shocked" (or titillated?) the clubmembers by "walking through the house not wearing a shirt!" Despite the Nobel Prize and his other considerable achievements, this remained throughout the years my mother's dominant image of the greatest writer of our century. My mother was fond of Estelle Faulkner, appreciating her warmth and vibrancy and her intense, "expectant" quality, and she observed once that Estelle "always looked as though she had just been rather surprised by something."

In 1936 when I was born, my parents lived on Fillmore Avenue in a small brick house that faced north but that backed on to open land leading into Bailey's Woods, a tract that Faulkner owned and that led south to Rowan Oak. Separated by these woods, Faulkner's grand house and my parents' modest bungalow lay less than a mile apart. In that same year, in Oxford and Los Angeles, Faulkner completed *Absalom, Absalom!* which was published on October 26. I was born two days later on October 28. So, Taylor (if you will indulge me here in a bit of hubris), it has always pleased me to recall that *Absalom* and I were gestating a short distance apart at exactly the same time. *Absalom, Absalom!* is much, much more important than I am, and it is surely my favorite Faulkner novel for reasons that are larger than the simultaneity of our births. Yet I enjoy remembering that I was born in good company.

After completing his master's degree, my father was faced with a choice of whether to go elsewhere to pursue a Ph.D. in classics and history or to stay in Mississippi and to continue, as teacher and administrator, to make whatever contributions he could to Mississippi public education. He chose the latter path, of course, with, I believe, considerable success in very difficult times, but I wonder sometimes if he should not have chosen the other option since he was undoubtedly a splendid teacher and had enormous, if underdeveloped, talent as a writer—talents that might have brought him more satisfaction, and certainly more approbation, than he received in the career he chose. In pursuit of that vocation, however, he left Oxford in 1937 to become superintendent of the schools of Como, Mississippi—an event of considerable importance to you, Taylor, since one of the first teachers he hired (and introduced to the town's most eligible bachelor, Ernest Taylor) was your future grandmother, Dorothy McGee. While in Como, my father remembered, he saw William Faulkner only once—at a barbecue given by Don and Maybelle Bartlett, your grandfather Taylor's first cousins. As before, my father recalled, he and Faulkner talked about Ripley as well as about Malcolm and Cho-Cho.

In 1940, TSH was offered a better and more demanding job as superintendent of the larger school system of Kosciusko in Attala County, Mississippi, where we lived for twelve years. There, among other old Kosciusko natives, we knew the Niles family, related to Estelle Oldham Faulkner. Through this connection, Faulkner must have become acquainted with aspects of the history and the character of Attala County, which while different in some ways from Tippah and Lafayette counties in north Mississippi, still has many resemblances to that "mythical" composite that Faulkner called "Yoknapatawpha."

The years we spent in Kosciusko during the forties and early fifties were the years when we returned most often to visit relatives and friends in Ripley and Oxford, and it was sometime in this period that I remember being in Memphis with my parents and going with my father to pay a visit to "Miss Bama" Falkner McLean, whom he had known all of his life. I must have been in my early teens because I had just finished reading *Intruder in the Dust,* and I was awed by the fact that this grand but friendly woman was the *daughter* of Colonel Falkner. I recall that she and my father talked about Ripley, of course, and that she spoke warmly not only of my grandparents but of my Spight and Hines *great*-grandparents. I remember thinking she was an ancient relic then, but she lived on, incredibly, until 1968, dying at the ripe age of ninety-four.

In 1952, my father was offered the position of Director of Admissions at Ole Miss, and we moved back to Oxford. Later, he became Director of Student Activities, a job he held until his retirement in 1972, the year before his death. I attended University High School for my junior and senior years and recall first seeing William Faulkner walking up North Lamar Street to the square, where he would frequently stand alone, smoking his pipe and looking into the distance. At other times, less often, I would observe him talking quietly to someone. The first time I remember actually meeting him and speaking with him was probably during my junior year in high school when his step-granddaughter, Vicki Fielden, Cho-Cho's daughter, visited the Faulkners with a roommate from school, and my friend and classmate William Lewis and I were asked to take them out. On this and the several other occasions when we did this, Faulkner would receive us and talk with us for the minutes we were waiting for the girls. I also remember that once the Faulkners hosted a dance for Vicki in the ballroom of The Mansion, a downtown restaurant. Both of them attended and were in good form. Sometime later when I ran into him once in the Kroger grocery store downtown, I asked him what he had heard from Vicki, who at that time had acting aspirations. "Vicki writes," he said drolly, "that she has a part in a play Off Broadway. But from what I can tell, it's pretty *far* off Broadway."

In the fall of 1954, I entered Ole Miss and met a fellow freshman from Little Rock, Arkansas: Dean Faulkner, the daughter of William's deceased younger brother, Dean, who had been killed in 1935 in a plane crash near Oxford, several months before his daughter was born. From that time on, William had assumed the role of avuncular, if unofficial, guardian. Dean called him "Pappy." Most of the rest of us called him Mr. Faulkner. It was, in fact, during my Ole Miss years, as a result of my being a classmate of Dean's, that I was privileged to be with Faulkner on a number of occasions, chiefly at Rowan Oak when Dean had parties there. Sometimes these gatherings were held while WF was away at the University of Virginia and while, I believe, his sister-in-law, Dorothy Oldham, was living at Rowan Oak as hostess and custodian. During our senior year, in the spring of 1958, when Dean became engaged to Jon Mallard, the Faulkners hosted a number of events to celebrate the occasion.

The timing, and the distinction between, these social events are now somewhat blurred in my memory, but I have no trouble recalling the specific conversations I had with Faulkner—mainly because by that time I had become such an admirer of his work and was so frankly awed by him and pleased that I was having a chance to talk with him. Because of this, I was also becoming more intrigued with the Ripley connections, though I was then much less knowledgeable of the details than I would later become. I regret, in retrospect, that we somehow never really talked about Ripley. Also, at that time, I had not yet read *Light in August,* and my greatest regret is that I did not know to ask him why he had chosen to give the noble name of Hines to one of his most despicable characters.

From those random occasions in the mid and late 1950s when I talked with William Faulkner, I recall the following exchanges: Once when I went to say good night and thank him for the evening, he replied with friendly mock-astonishment: "Well, Tom, I am sorry you are leaving; I didn't realize we were out of liquor." I also recall with particular vividness the engagement party he gave for Dean and Jon in the garden at Rowan Oak when he stood with them on the east porch and made the only truly "Faulknerian" speech I ever heard him make. It recalled phrases and sentiments of other statements of his that I had read or heard on taped soundtracks, including echoes even of the Nobel Prize address. I remember Faulkner's version of that ancient meditation on youth and age to the effect that ". . . those of us here with a lot of white hair and maybe even a little more wisdom as a result of the white hair, admire and envy your youth and energy and optimism even if you don't yet have the wisdom that you will get later. . . ."—or something like that.

Following a Saturday morning brunch at Rowan Oak just prior to Dean's wedding, as we prepared to leave for an Ole Miss football game, I reminded Mr. Faulkner that we had extra tickets and urged him to join us. "Well, thank you, Tom," he replied, in declining the invitation, "but I've never liked professional football or amateur show business."

I also recall that at one of the wedding functions, I had a good visit with Lucile and John Faulkner, William's brother. John was a long-time acquaintance and golfing partner of my father's. And on that particular occasion, he was especially cordial and voluble and talked at length about Ripley, his birthplace, and about the several generations of my family he had known there. The night before the wedding, following the rehearsal dinner—since Jon Mallard had no headquarters in Oxford—I offered my apartment, beneath my parents' garage, as the site for the obligatory "bachelors' party." About twelve of Dean's and Jon's male friends and relatives were present, including William Faulkner, who drove over with me as we preceded the other guests.

As I was preparing the bar, I rather matter-of-factly put a record on the phonograph, which must have struck him as inappropriate for this manly occasion, and I will never forget his firm request to "please turn that thing off." Faulkner had apparently decided not to drink at most of these social events, but here I recall he did have a glass of bourbon, and perhaps more than one. For this, or for other reasons in the spirit of the occasion, he became more talkative than I had ever heard him and I seem to recall that, in one round of rather rowdy joke-telling, he also told a funny joke, the gist of which neither I nor anyone else who was present could remember later—since the rest of us had far, far more to drink than he did. I regret to say that while I recall having a very good time, I remember *nothing* else about the evening.

Following the wedding and graduation and Dean's departure from Oxford, and before I left the next year to go into the Army, I had several pleasant and interesting encounters with Mr. F. I had *thought* that after the Army I wanted to get a Ph.D., but I was not certain yet that I really wanted to spend my life teaching and writing history, and so I decided to take a year's deferment, do a master's degree at Ole Miss, teach a freshman survey course and see how I liked it before making a full commitment to graduate work elsewhere. I did a master's thesis on the movement in Mississippi to repeal the states's prohibition laws in the twenties and thirties, and I discovered in my research that, in the early 1930s, Faulkner had been a member and even an officer of a pro-repeal organization, called The Crusaders. One evening I saw him downtown at The Mansion restaurant, where he was having dinner, and I asked him to tell me what he could remember about The Crusaders. He replied that frankly he could not remember very much about that noble effort except that it was clearly something he had gotten excited over and "signed my name to one hot summer night over a bottle of gin." He also mused, in those still "dry" days in Mississippi, that The Crusaders had obviously not been immediately successful.

In that same year at Ole Miss, I had been elected president of a history student honor society, the Claiborne Society, and had announced to my faculty mentors, James Silver and John Moore, that I intended to ask Faulkner to speak to the group on some rather grand topic like "the relationship of history and fiction." They laughed politely at my naivete and warned me not to be disappointed when he said no. Silver had apparently invited him to speak to students a number of times without success. But I still went confidently down to Rowan Oak to invite him anyway. He came to the door, greeted me cordially, and we sat on his front porch and discussed the matter. He asked about the size of the group, and I assured him it would be small. We then talked about potential times and locations, and lo and behold, he said yes. He wanted minimal publicity and assurance that there would be, for the most part, only students there, and since the event was to take place several months hence, he asked me to come back the week before and remind him personally since, he warned me, he frequently did not answer the phone. I agreed to do that and to come for him the day of the talk and drive him to the campus.

Back at Ole Miss, Silver and Moore were somewhat flabbergasted, but impressed that I had been able to get him to agree to speak. We made modest arrangements for the event and I went back the week before it to remind him and to make final arrangements. He answered the door, seemed somewhat distant and distracted, and when I mentioned the talk, he said: "Oh, yes. . . . Well, Tom, I'll have to ask you to give me a rain check this time. I'm working now, and I can't stop for this." I was, of course, dejected and was chagrined to think of having to tell my mentors what had happened. They, in their wisdom, were not surprised. I realized only slowly, of course, that when he told me he was "working," he meant that his writing was going well. Since this was 1959, he was probably working on *The Reivers*. For me, it was another interesting glimpse into his world even if it meant no talk to the Claiborne Society.

One of my greatest pleasures in Oxford in the 1950s was getting to know Faulkner's mother, "Miss Maud," who had been a friend of my grandmother's in Ripley in the early twentieth century. When I knew her, she was in her mid-eighties. After Dean left, during the last year I was in Oxford, I became Mrs. Falkner's library courier, stopping by every week or so to visit with her and to return or deliver the books that she had asked me to check out for her from the Ole Miss library. Blotner's edition of the *Selected Letters* (p. 442) includes a brief mention by Faulkner of my and his mother's book-swapping relationship. During that year, Maud Falkner was reading through the Russian giants, Tolstoy, Dostoevsky, Chekhov, and Turgenev. She spoke very knowledgeably and enthusiastically about her literary interests, including the work of William Faulkner and his critics, about which she was richly informed. She delighted in finding errors in the critics' pieces. One of these had identified Maud Falkner as William's *grand*mother. Though she usually spoke quietly, her voice rose as she laughed at that. "Of course, William Faulkner is over sixty years old," she said, "and when anyone speaks of Faulkner's mother, people say: 'Faulkner's *mother?* Is *she* still alive?' But now this man is trying to make me even older than I am."

As an avid reader and as a loyal mother, she also admired the comic talent of her son John, particularly his novel *Men Working,* and she regretted that his fate of standing in the shadow of his brother made his work less appreciated than she felt it should have been. She also enjoyed popular best sellers. Once when we were discussing some high literary matter, she paused, smiled, and asked if I could guess what her favorite "bedtime novel" was. "Promise you won't tell anybody," she said. "It's Herman Wouk's *The Caine Mutiny!*"

Mrs. Falkner was also a good, amateur, small-town painter, and when I went by to say goodbye to her as I left Oxford in early 1960, she gave me a variant of a portrait she had done of an old black man in Oxford named "Preacher Green." An earlier variant hangs at Rowan Oak and was much loved by Faulkner. Maud Falkner was a warm and wise person, whose sophisticated intellect has never been sufficiently appreciated even by the most gifted Faulkner interpreters. Occasionally on my weekly visits with her, I would encounter Faulkner, coming or going. He and she were clearly devoted to each other and owed each other considerable debts. He was concerned about her living alone and he asked me one day when we met at her house if I would try to find an Ole Miss graduate student who might be willing to stay there for room rent and be available if she needed anything. I found the ideal candidate, a mature, unobtrusive graduate student in English whom Faulkner approved. Yet when he broached this to Miss Maud, she firmly declined the proposal. As fiercely private as Faulkner himself was, she remained independent to the end. She died in 1960, less than a year after I left Oxford.

Shortly before I left, I drove out to Sardis Lake one cold winter afternoon and passed Faulkner returning in his jeep. We waved to each other. In 1962, I was stationed in Germany but vacationing in Luxembourg when I read of his death in the *International Herald-Tribune.* Shortly before that, my parents had seen him and talked with him briefly at a party at Bill and Mary Moore Green's; he had fallen from his horse and was clearly not feeling well. When I read of Faulkner's death and then received clippings from my family about his funeral, I recalled that, sometime in the 1950s, I had overheard my parents talking about where they wanted to be buried. Should it be in the Ripley cemetery with all the Spights and Hineses or in Oxford where they planned to live the rest of their lives? They decided on Oxford, and my father went down to the courthouse to purchase a plot. When he returned, he said, "Well, guess who I ran into at the courthouse doing the same thing I was doing? William Faulkner!" They apparently spoke, with appropriate levity, about this fateful step they were both taking. Several generations of Faulkner's family had, of course, been buried in Oxford, but the original plot was filled and WF was assigned another one for his own family in the newer part of St. Peter's. Faulkner had arrived at the clerk's office first and was leaving as TSH arrived. Since my father was next in line, he was assigned, in good bureaucratic fashion, the next plot due east of the Faulkners. Both of my parents' graves are there now, along with that of my younger sister Polly Pope Hines, who died in infancy and whose grave was removed to Oxford from Ripley, where she was first buried in 1941. Sally and I will someday be buried there with them. As with *Absalom, Absalom!* I will again consider myself in good company—for eternity.

After I left Germany and the army in 1963, I spent five years working for my Ph.D. at the University of Wisconsin in Madison. There and at UCLA, where I started teaching in 1968, I felt, with the exception of family and close friends, rather disaffected from Mississippi culture, a distancing that probably also tempered my earlier enthusiasm for Faulkner. It was only in the 1980s, when Ann Abadie, at the Ole Miss Center for the Study of Southern Culture, asked me to lead a Lafayette County architecture tour at the annual August Faulkner conference and then later to develop a lecture on "The Architecture of Yoknapatawpha," that I got really interested again in Faulkner and his world— my world. This overly long letter should prove to you that I am clearly still interested, perhaps more than "interested," in this complicated place, the American South. Faulkner's art, of course, while getting at the South more trenchantly than anyone else has ever done, goes far beyond it (as he uses it metaphorically) to embrace and interpret what he himself once called "the comedy and tragedy of being alive." I will follow with interest, Taylor, your own journey through Yoknapatawpha, and hope that these words will interest you.

Love, Dad

Preface

1. Faulkner used these words in an Associated Press radio news bulletin, following the death of Ernest Hemingway on July 2, 1961, almost exactly a year before Faulkner's own death. I have never seen the statement published, but I vividly recall hearing it on the broadcast. Faulkner's tribute dealt, in effect, with Hemingway's ability to capture in words "the comedy and tragedy of being alive."

Introduction

1. William Faulkner, *Mosquitoes* (New York: Boni and Liveright, 1927), pp. 106–7.

2. Eudora Welty, "Place in Fiction," *The Eye of the Story* (New York: Random House, 1978), pp. 118–19; Malcolm Cowley, "Introduction," *The Portable Faulkner* (1946; New York: Viking, 1951), p. 5.

3. William T. Ruzicka, *Faulkner's Fictive Architecture: The Meaning of Place in the Yoknapatawpha Novels* (Ann Arbor: University of Michigan Press, 1987), p. 2. This short, insightful analysis by a literary scholar focuses on the neoclassical architecture in Faulkner's novels. Besides my own work, Ruzicka's is virtually the only other study that treats the subject at all.

4. Joel Williamson, *William Faulkner and Southern History* (New York: Oxford University Press, 1993), p. 413.

5. Hayden White, "The Fictions of Factual Representation," *Tropics of Discourse: Essays in Cultural Criticism* (Baltimore: The Johns Hopkins University Press, 1978), p. 122; Erik H. Erikson, "Psychological Reality and Historical Actuality," *Insight and Responsibility: Lectures on the Ethical Implications of Psychoanalytic Insight* (New York: W. W. Norton, 1964), p. 159.

6. Faulkner, "Monk," *Knight's Gambit* (1949; New York: Vintage Books, 1978), p. 39; Faulkner, *The Town* (1957; New York: Vintage Books, 1961), p. 88.

7. Elizabeth M. Kerr, *Yoknapatawpha: Faulkner's "Little Postage Stamp of Native Soil"* (New York: Fordham University Press, 1969), p. 11, quoting Faulkner from Frederick L. Gwynn and Joseph Blotner, eds., *Faulkner in the University* (Charlottesville: University Press of Virginia, 1959), p. 84.

8. Gaston Bachelard, *The Poetics of Space* (Boston: Beacon Press, 1969), p. 8; Faulkner, *Sartoris* (1929; New York: Signet, 1957), p. 74.

9. Conversation with Patricia Brown Young, Oxford, Mississippi, May 8, 1995; for a slightly different version, see Maggie Brown, "Hunt Breakfast, Faulkner Style," in James W. Webb and A. Wigfall Green, eds., *William Faulkner of Oxford* (Baton Rouge: Louisiana State University Press, 1965), pp. 122–23.

1. *"The Purlieus of Elegance"*

1. Ben Wasson, *Count No 'Count: Flashbacks to Faulkner* (Jackson: University Press of Mississippi, 1983), pp. 54–55.

2. Joseph Blotner, *Faulkner: A Biography* (New York: Random House, 1974), vol. 1, pp. 443–83.

3. Ibid., p. 443.

4. Faulkner, *Sanctuary* (1931; New York: Vintage Books, 1958), p. 308.

5. Faulkner, *Mosquitoes,* pp. 10, 14.

6. Faulkner, *Absalom, Absalom!* (1936; New York: Vintage Books, 1972), p. 110.

7. Blotner, *Faulkner,* vol. 1, p. 415; Faulkner, Interview with Jean Stein, *Paris Review,* Spring 1956; reprinted in James B. Meriwether and Michael Millgate, eds., *Lion in the Garden: Interviews with William Faulkner, 1926–1962* (Lincoln: University of Nebraska Press, 1968), p. 255.

2. *"A Just and Holy Cause"*

1. Faulkner, *Sartoris,* p. 143.

2. Faulkner, *Requiem for a Nun* (1950; New York: Vintage Books, 1975), pp. 206–7.

3. Faulkner, *Sartoris,* p. 299.

3. *"Of Secret and Violent Blood"*

1. Lewis M. Dabney, *The Indians of Yoknapatawpha: A Study in Literature and History* (Baton Rouge: Louisiana State University Press, 1974), pp. 3–42.

2. Ibid.; Faulkner, "Mississippi," *Holiday,* April 1954, p. 35.

3. Faulkner, "A Bear Hunt," *Collected Stories of William Faulkner* (New York: Random House, 1950), p. 65.

4. In Dabney, *The Indians of Yoknapatawpha,* cited above, p. 24, Faulkner is quoted as stating both in Japan (Meriwether and Millgate, *Lion in the Garden: Interviews with William Faulkner,* pp. 133–134) and at the University of Virginia (*Faulkner in the University,* p. 74), that Yoknapatawpha meant "slowly moving water" or "water flowing slow through the flat land," which I quoted in the first printing of this book. I am grateful to John Pritchard, Memphis, Tennessee, for referring me to Pamela Munro and Catherine Willmond, *Chickasaw, An Analytical Dictionary,* (Norman and London: The University of Oklahoma, 1994), pp. 299, 359, which corrects Faulkner's translation and instead defines "yaakni" as "ground, earth, land, property, country," and "pataffi" (and its variant, "patafa") as "to rip, to slash, cut open, disembowel." The compound form likely referred to the river, itself, as "slashing" or "cutting open" the land.

4. *"Alien Yet Inviolably Durable"*

1. James A. Latham III, *Mississippi Folk Houses,* pamphlet (Washington, D.C.: National Endowment for the Humanities, 1977), pp. 5–8.

2. Ibid.

3. Ibid.; Charles B. Cramer, "A History of Selected Examples of Ante-Bellum Architecture in Lafayette County, Mississippi," unpublished ms., University of Mississippi Art Department, 1965, Mississippi Collection, John Davis Williams Library, University of Mississippi, Oxford; Jack Case Wilson, *Faulkners, Fortunes, and Flames* (Nashville: Annandale Press, 1984), p. 51.

4. Faulkner, *The Mansion* (1955; New York: Vintage Books, 1965), pp. 398—99.

5. Faulkner, *The Hamlet* (1940; New York: Vintage Books, 1956), pp. 219, 257; Michael Millgate, *The Achievement of William Faulkner* (Lincoln: University of Nebraska Press, 1978), pp. 192—93.

6. Ibid.

7. Faulkner, *As I Lay Dying* (1930; New York: The Modern Library, 1946), p. 339.

8. Faulkner, *Knight's Gambit,* pp. 240—41.

9. Faulkner, "1699—1945, The Compsons," appendix to Cowley, ed., *The Portable Faulkner,* p. 737.

10. Faulkner, "Barn Burning," *Collected Stories,* p. 3.

11. Faulkner, *The Hamlet,* pp. 84—85; 78; Faulkner, "1699—1945, The Compsons," pp. 745—46.

12. Faulkner, *The Sound and the Fury* (1929; New York: The Modern Library, 1946), pp. 307—8.

5. *"The Aspirations and the Hopes"*

1. Leland Roth, *A Concise History of American Architecture* (New York: Harper and Row, 1979), p. 53.

2. R. Furneau Jordan, *A Concise History of Western Architecture* (New York: Harcourt, Brace and World, 1970), pp. 46—47.

3. Wasson, *Count No 'Count,* p. 55.

4. Catherine Bishir, *North Carolina Architecture* (Chapel Hill: University of North Carolina Press, 1990), p. 163.

5. Faulkner, *Requiem for a Nun,* p. 35.

6. Ibid, p. 34.

7. Ibid.

8. Ibid., pp. 39—40; Hardeman County [Tennessee] Historical Commission, *Hardeman County Historical Sketches* (N.p.: Taylor Publishing Company, 1979), p. 2.

9. Wilson, *Faulkners, Fortunes, and Flames,* p. 78. This corrects the frequently asserted claim that Turner was "English," an idea apparently accepted by Faulkner himself.

10. Cramer, "Ante-Bellum Architecture," pp. 25—26.

11. Ibid.

12. Ibid., pp. 26—28.

13. John Faulkner, *My Brother Bill: An Affectionate Remniscence* (New York: Trident Press, 1963), pp. 271—73; Wilson, *Faulkners, Fortunes, and Flames,* pp. 66—69.

14. Cramer, "Ante-Bellum Architecture," pp. 9—11; 16—17.

15. Ibid., pp. 14—15; Susan Snell, *Phil Stone of Oxford: A Vicarious Life* (Athens: University of Georgia Press, 1991), pp. 21—24.

16. Cramer, "Ante-Bellum Architecture," pp. 17—22.

17. Ibid.

18. John Pilkington, *Stark Young* (Boston: Twayne, 1985); Stark Young, *The Pavilion: Of People and Times Remembered, Of Stories and Places* (New York: Charles Scribner's Sons, 1951).

19. Pilkington, *Stark Young,* pp. 75—87; Young, *The Pavilion,* p. 96.

20. Pilkington, *Stark Young,* pp. 87—98.

21. Faulkner, *Sanctuary,* pp. 7—8, 18.

22. Faulkner, *The Hamlet,* pp. 5–6.

23. Faulkner, "Barn Burning," p. 10.

24. Faulkner, *Knight's Gambit,* p. 143.

25. Faulkner, *Sartoris,* p. 303.

26. Ibid., pp. 23–24.

27. Faulkner, *Absalom, Absalom!,* pp. 9, 69; Faulkner, *Requiem for a Nun,* p. 35.

28. Ruzicka, *Faulkner's Fictive Architecture,* p. 45.

29. Faulkner, *Absalom, Absalom!,* pp. 36–38.

30. Ibid.

31. Ibid., p. 256.

32. Ibid., p. 85.

33. Ibid., pp. 136–37.

6. *"Immolated Sticks and Stones"*

1. *The Random House Dictionary of the English Language* (New York: Random House, 1967); Malcolm Cowley, *The Faulkner-Cowley File: Letters and Memories, 1944–1962* (1966; New York: Penguin, 1978), pp. 12–13.

2. Roth, *Concise History of American Architecture,* pp. 110–12.

3. Ibid.; Mary Alice Crocker, *Historic Architecture in Mississippi* (Jackson: University Press of Mississippi, 1973), p. 150.

4. James B. Lloyd, *The University of Mississippi, The Formative Years, 1848–1906. Catalogue of an Exhibition Held at the Library of the University of Mississippi* (Oxford: University of Mississippi Art Museum, 1979), pp. 10–11.

5. Faulkner, *Absalom, Absalom!,* p. 56.

6. Faulkner, *Knight's Gambit,* p. 241.

7. Faulkner, *The Town,* p. 306.

8. Roth, *Concise History of American Architecture,* pp. 101–4; Wayne Andrews, *Architecture, Ambition, and Americans: A Social History of American Architecture* (Toronto: Free Press, 1964), pp. 106–9.

9. Faulkner, *Sartoris,* pp. 145–46.

10. Cramer, "Ante-Bellum Architecture," pp. 29–30; Andrew Jackson Downing, *The Architecture of Country Houses* (New York: Da Capo Press, 1968), p. 380.

11. Cramer, "Ante-Bellum Architecture," pp. 29–33.

7. *"A Kind of Majesty"*

1. Wilson, *Faulkners, Fortunes, and Flames,* pp. 22–24; 81. A later owner changed the name to "Ammadelle."

2. Ibid., pp. 48–49.

3. I am grateful to Taylor Pointer, Dorothy Taylor Hines, and other members of their family for sharing the details of this story with me.

4. Wilson, *Faulkners, Fortunes, and Flames,* pp. 82–85.

5. Ibid., p. 95.

6. Faulkner, *The Sound and the Fury,* p. 161.

7.   Donald Philip Duclos, "Son of Sorrow: The Life, Works, and Influence of Colonel William C. Falkner, 1825–1889" (Ph.D. diss., University of Michigan, 1962), pp. 268, 286.

8.   The *Jackson Clarion,* quoted in Blotner, *Faulkner,* vol. 1, p. 41; Andrew Brown, *History of Tippah County, Mississippi: The First Century* (Ripley: The Tippah County Historical and Genealogical Society, n.d.), p. 290; Duclos, "Son of Sorrow," p. 286. See also Jane Isbell Haynes, *William Faulkner: His Tippah County Heritage: Lands, Houses, and Businesses, Ripley, Mississippi* (Columbia, S.C.: The Seajay Press, 1985), pp. 1–34.

9.   When Falkner's daughter Willie Carter left Ripley in the early twentieth century, she sold the house to her friend (and cousin of Holland Pearce Falkner) Mattie Spight Hines and Mattie's husband, William—my grandparents. At about this same time, the Falkner heirs sold Colonel Falkner's house to another Spight cousin, Lynn Donelson Spight, my great-uncle, and gave the alligator to my father's family, who now lived in the old Carter house.

10. Faulkner, *Sartoris,* pp. 36–37.

11. Elizabeth Spencer, "Emerging as a Writer in Faulkner's Mississippi," paper given at the "Faulkner and Yoknapatawpha" Conference at the University of Mississippi, August 1982; Faulkner, "A Rose for Emily," *Collected Stories,* p. 119.

12. Faulkner, *Intruder in the Dust* (New York: Random House, 1948), pp. 49–50.

8. *"Spacious, Suave, Sonorous, and Monastic"*

1.   Conversations with Robert Canizaro, Jackson, Mississippi, and Henry Mitchell, Oxford, Mississippi, August 1995.

2.   Ward L. Miner, *The World of William Faulkner* (New York: Grove Press, 1952), p. 63; Faulkner, *Sanctuary,* p. 6.

3.   Faulkner, *Pylon* (1935; New York: Random House, 1962), pp. 37–38. Though Faulkner completed *Pylon* before the new main building at the Memphis airport was built, he would have known the older, adjacent, and even more "modernist" hangars that pre-dated it.

4.   Faulkner, *The Sound and the Fury,* p. 99.

5.   Faulkner, "Dull Tale," Joseph Blotner, ed., *Uncollected Stories of William Faulkner* (New York, Vintage Books, 1981), p. 529.

6.   Conversation with Ella Sommerville, Oxford, Mississippi, ca. 1958.

7.   Faulkner, "Mississippi," p. 44.

8.   Faulkner, *Sanctuary,* p. 118.

9.   Blotner, *Faulkner,* vol. 1, pp. 550, 1069, 1084, 1227; Faulkner, *Requiem for a Nun,* p. 41.

10. Faulkner, *Requiem for a Nun,* p. 210.

11. Faulkner, "Golden Land," *Collected Stories,* p. 719.

12. Faulkner, *The Mansion,* p. 154; Faulkner, *The Town,* p. 352.

13. Faulkner, *Requiem for a Nun,* p. 215.

9. *Conclusion*

1.   Faulkner, *Sartoris,* pp. 142–43.

2.   Faulkner, *The Sound and the Fury,* pp. 335–36.

SELECTED BIBLIOGRAPHY

Works Consulted in the Preparation of This Volume

Works by William Faulkner (in order of first publication)

NOVELS

Mosquitoes. New York: Boni and Liveright, 1927.

Sartoris. 1929; New York: Signet, 1957.

The Sound and the Fury. 1929; New York: The Modern Library, 1946.

As I Lay Dying. 1930; New York: The Modern Library, 1946.

Sanctuary. 1931; New York: Vintage Books, 1958.

Pylon. 1935; New York: Random House, 1962.

Absalom, Absalom! 1936; New York: Vintage Books, 1972.

The Hamlet. 1940; New York: Vintage Books, 1956.

Intruder in the Dust. New York: Random House, 1948.

Knight's Gambit. 1949; New York: Vintage Books, 1978.

Requiem for a Nun. 1950; New York: Vintage Books, 1975.

The Mansion. 1955; New York: Vintage Books, 1965.

The Town. 1957; New York: Vintage Books, 1961.

FAULKNER: SHORT STORIES

"A Bear Hunt," "Barn Burning," "A Rose for Emily," and "Golden Land." In *Collected Stories of William Faulkner.* New York: Random House, 1950.

"Dull Tale." In *Uncollected Stories of William Faulkner,* edited by Joseph Blotner. New York: Vintage Books, 1981.

FAULKNER: MISCELLANEOUS

"1699—1945, The Compsons." Appendix to *The Portable Faulkner,* edited by Malcolm Cowley. New York: Viking, 1946.

"Mississippi." *Holiday,* April 1954.

Interview with Jean Stein. *Paris Review,* Spring 1956. Reprinted in *Lion in the Garden: Interviews With William Faulkner, 1926–1962,* edited by James B. Meriwether and Michael Millgate. Lincoln: University of Nebraska Press, 1968.

Selected Letters of William Faulkner. Edited by Joseph Blotner. New York: Random House, 1977.

Faulkner and Southern Literary Studies

A. I. Bezzerides. *William Faulkner: A Life on Paper.* Adapted and edited by Ann Abadie. Jackson: University Press of Mississippi, 1980.

Joseph Blotner. *Faulkner: A Biography.* Two volumes. New York: Random House, 1974.

Jack Cofield. *William Faulkner: The Cofield Collection.* Oxford, Miss.: Yoknapatawpha Press, 1978.

Robert Coughlan. *The Private World of William Faulkner: The Man, The Legend, The Writer.* New York: Harper, 1953.

Malcolm Cowley. Introduction to *The Portable Faulkner.* New York: Viking , 1946.

————. *The Faulkner-Cowley File: Letters and Memories, 1944–1962.* 1966; New York: Penguin, 1978.

John B. Cullen, in collaboration with Floyd C. Watkins. *Old Times in the Faulkner Country.* Chapel Hill: University of North Carolina Press, 1961.

Lewis M. Dabney. *The Indians of Yoknapatawpha: A Study in Literature and History.* Baton Rouge: Louisiana State University Press, 1974.

Martin J. Dain. *Faulkner's County: Yoknapatawpha.* New York: Random House, 1963.

Donald Philip Duclos. "Son of Sorrow: The Life, Works, and Influence of Colonel William C. Falkner, 1825–1889." Ph.D. diss., University of Michigan, 1962.

John Faulkner. *My Brother Bill: An Affectionate Remniscence.* New York: Trident Press, 1963.

Frederick L. Gwynn and Joseph Blotner, eds. *Faulkner in the University.* Charlottesville: University Press of Virginia, 1959.

Jane Isbell Haynes. *William Faulkner: His Tippah County Heritage: Lands, Houses and Businesses, Ripley, Mississippi.* Columbia, S.C.: The Seejay Press, 1985.

————. *William Faulkner: His Lafayette County Heritage: Lands, Houses and Businesses, Oxford, Mississippi.* Ripley, Miss.: Tippah County Historical and Genealogical Society, 1992.

Irving Howe. *William Faulkner: A Critical Study.* Chicago: University of Chicago Press, 1975.

Elizabeth M. Kerr. *Yoknapatawpha: Faulkner's "Little Postage Stamp of Native Soil."* New York: Fordham University Press, 1969.

John Lawrence and Dan Hise. *Faulkner's Rowan Oak.* Jackson: University Press of Mississippi, 1993.

Michael Millgate. *The Achievement of William Faulkner.* Lincoln: University of Nebraska Press, 1978.

Ward L. Miner. *The World of William Faulkner.* New York: Grove Press, 1952.

Willie Morris and William Eggleston. *Faulkner's Mississippi.* Birmingham, Ala.: Oxmoor House, 1990.

John Pilkington. *The Heart of Yoknapatawpha.* Jackson: University Press of Mississippi, 1981.

————. *Stark Young.* Boston: Twayne, 1985.

William T. Ruzicka. *Faulkner's Fictive Architecture: The Meaning of Place in the Yoknapatawpha Novels.* Ann Arbor: University of Michigan Press, 1987.

Susan Snell. *Phil Stone of Oxford: A Vicarious Life.* Athens: University of Georgia Press, 1991.

Elizabeth Spencer. "Emerging as a Writer in Faulkner's Mississippi." Paper given at the "Faulkner and Yoknapatawpha" Conference, University of Mississippi, Oxford, August 1982.

Herman E. Taylor. *Faulkner's Oxford: Recollections and Reflections.* Nashville, Tenn.: Rutledge Hill Press, 1990.

Ben Wasson. *Count No 'Count: Flashbacks to Faulkner.* Jackson: University Press of Mississippi, 1983.

James W. Webb and A. Wigfall Green, eds. *William Faulkner of Oxford.* Baton Rouge: Louisiana State University Press, 1965.

Joel Williamson. *William Faulkner and Southern History.* New York: Oxford University Press, 1993.

Stark Young. *Heaven Trees.* New York: Charles Scribner's Sons, 1926.

———. *The Torches Flare.* New York: Charles Scribner's Sons, 1928.

———. *River House.* New York: Charles Scribner's Sons, 1929.

———. *So Red the Rose.* New York: Charles Scribner's Sons, 1934.

———. *The Pavilion: Of People and Times Remembered, of Stories and Places.* New York: Charles Scribner's Sons, 1951.

Mississippi and Southern History

Andrew Brown. *History of Tippah County, Mississippi. The First Century.* Ripley: The Tippah County Historical and Genealogical Society, n.d.

Calvin S. Brown. *Archeology of Mississippi.* Oxford: University of Mississippi for the Mississippi Geological Survey, 1926.

Daughters of the American Revolution, David Reese Chapter. "Some Early History of Lafayette County, Mississippi." Unpublished ms. [ca. 1922]. Mississippi Collection, John Davis Williams Library, University of Mississippi, Oxford

Hardeman County [Tennessee] Historical Commission. *Hardeman County Historical Sketches.* N.p.: Taylor Publishing Company, 1979.

James B. Lloyd. *The University of Mississippi: The Formative Years, 1848–1906. Catalogue of an Exhibition Held at the Library of the University of Mississippi.* Oxford: University of Mississippi Art Museum, 1979.

James W. Loewen and Charles Sallis. *Mississippi: Conflict and Change.* New York: Pantheon, 1974.

Panola County Genealogical and Historical Society. *History of Panola County, Mississippi.* Dallas: Curtis Media Corporation, 1987.

C. John Sobotka, Jr. *A History of Lafayette County, Mississippi.* Oxford: Rebel Press, 1976.

Tippah County Historical and Genealogical Society. *The History of Tippah County, Mississippi.* Tulsa, Okla.: Heritage Publishing, 1981.

Jack Case Wilson. *Faulkners, Fortunes, and Flames.* Nashville: Annandale Press, 1984.

History of Architecture

Wayne Andrews. *Architecture, Ambition, and Americans: A Social History of American Architecture.* Toronto: Free Press, 1964.

Catherine Bishir. *North Carolina Architecture.* Chapel Hill: University of North Carolina Press, 1990.

Charles B. Cramer. "A History of Selected Examples of Ante-Bellum Architecture in Lafayette County, Mississippi." Unpublished paper, University of Mississippi Art Department, 1965; Mississippi Collection, John Davis Williams Library, University of Mississippi, Oxford.

Mary Alice Crocker. *Historic Architecture in Mississippi.* Jackson: University Press of Mississippi, 1973.

Andrew Jackson Downing. *The Architecture of Country Houses.* New York: Da Capo Press, 1968.

R. Furneau Jordan. *A Concise History of Western Architecture.* New York: Harcourt, Brace and World, 1970.

Mills Lane, *The Architecture of the Old South: Alabama and Mississippi.* New York: Abbeville Press, 1989.

James A. Latham III. *Mississippi Folk Houses.* Pamphlet. Washington, D.C.: National Endowment for the Humanities, 1977.

C. Ford Peatross and Robert O. Mellown. *William Nichols, Architect*. Tuscaloosa: University of Alabama Art Gallery, 1979.

Leland Roth. *A Concise History of American Architecture*. New York: Harper and Row, 1979.

J. Frazier Smith. *White Pillars: Early Life and Architecture of the Lower Mississippi Valley Country*. New York: Bramhall House, 1941.

Theoretical Studies

Gaston Bachelard. *The Poetics of Space*. Boston: Beacon Press, 1969.

Roland Barthes. *Camera Lucida: Reflections on Photography*. New York: Hill and Wang, 1981.

Kenneth Boulding. *The Image: Knowledge in Life and Society*. Ann Arbor: University of Michigan Press, 1956.

Erik H. Erikson. "Psychological Reality and Historical Actuality." *Insight and Responsibility: Lectures on the Ethical Implications of Psychoanalytic Insight*. New York: W. W. Norton, 1964.

Susan Sontag. *On Photography*. New York: Farrar, Straus and Giroux, 1973.

Eudora Welty. "Place in Fiction." *The Eye of the Story*. New York: Random House, 1978.

Hayden White. "The Fictions of Factual Representation." *Tropics of Discourse: Essays in Cultural Criticism*. Baltimore: Johns Hopkins University Press, 1978.

The Author: cover, endpapers, plates 2, 3, 4, 5, 6, 7, 8, 9, 10, figs. 3, 4, 5, 6, 9, 10, 11, 14, 16, 17, 18, 19, 20, 22, 23, 24, 25, 26, 27, 28, 29, 30, 31, 32, 33, 34, 37, 40, 41, 42, 45, 47, 48, 49, 50, 51, 52, 53, 54, 55, 56, 57, 58, 59, 60, 62, 63, 64, 65, 66, 67, 68, 69, 70, 71, 72, 75, 77, 80, 85, 89, 90, 91, 93, 95, 99.

Collection of the author: Frontispiece (gift of the photographer, J.R. Cofield, published with the subsequent permission of Jack Cofield), figs. 94, 100.

City of Oxford, Mississippi: plate 1, fig. 96.

J.R. Cofield Collection, Center for the Study of Southern Culture, University of Mississippi: figs. 1, 35, 36, 76.

W.J. Blasingame Collection, Oxford, Mississippi: figs. 2, 7 (photograph by Phil Mullen), 83, 84, 88, 92.

American Play Company, New York: fig. 8.

Calvin S. Brown, *Archaeology of Mississippi* (Oxford: University of Mississippi for the Mississippi Geological Survey, 1926): figs. 12, 13.

Martin Dain Collection, Center for the Study of Southern Culture, University of Mississippi: fig. 15.

Patricia Brown Young Collection, Oxford, Mississippi: figs. 21, 38, 78, 82.

Jack Case Wilson Collection, Nashville, Tennessee: figs. 39, 44.

Araminta Stone Johnson Collection, Charlotte, North Carolina: fig. 43.

Taylor Pointer Collection, Como, Mississippi (drawing by Ruffin Sledge Davis): fig. 46.

Dorothy Lee Tatum Collection, Oxford, Mississippi: fig. 61.

Ripley Public Library, Ripley, Mississippi: figs. 73, 74, 98, 102.

B.B. Bradley, Columbia, Mississippi: fig. 79.

Robert Canizaro Collection, Jackson, Mississippi: fig. 81.

Memphis Area Chamber of Commerce, Memphis, Tennessee: fig. 86.

United States Army Corps of Engineers, Vicksburg District, fig. 87.

Mattie Spight McDowell Collection, Improve, Mississippi: fig. 101.

James W. Loewen and Charles Sallis, editors, *Mississippi: Conflict and Change* (New York: Pantheon Books, 1974): fig. 97.

INDEX

Compositor: G & S Typesetters
Text and Display: Perpetua
Printer: Malloy Lithographing
Binder: Malloy Lithographing

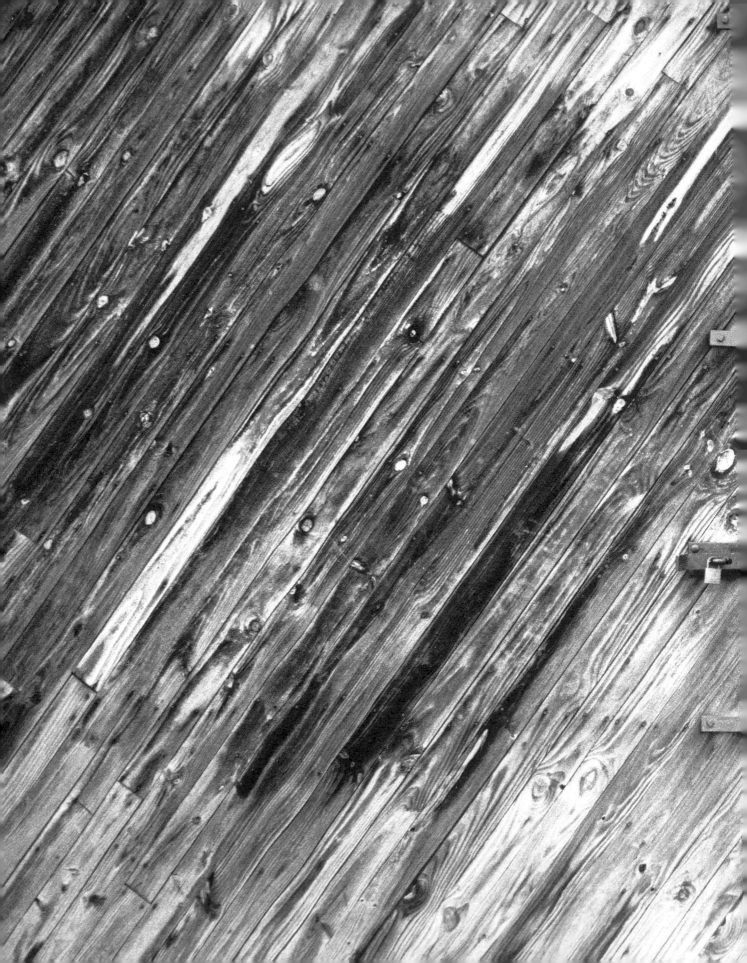